Skeptic in the House of God

Skeptic in the House of God

James L. Kelley

 Rutgers University Press
New Brunswick, New Jersey, and London

Library of Congress Cataloging-in-Publication Data

Kelley, James L., 1935–
        Skeptic in the house of God / James L. Kelley.
            p.   cm.
        Includes bibliographical references.
        ISBN 0-8135-2427-X (alk. paper)
            1. Kelley, James L., 1935–   —Religion.   2. Agnostics—Washington
        (D.C.)—Biography.   3. St. Mark's Church (Washington, D.C. :
        (Episcopal)   I. Title.
        BL2790.K45A3   1997
        211′.7′092—dc21   97-2377
        [B]   CIP

British Cataloging-in-Publication information available

Excerpts from "The Love Song of J. Alfred Prufrock" and "Ash Wednesday" from *Collected Poems 1901–1962* by T. S. Eliot, copyright 1936 by Harcourt Brace & Company, copyright 1964, 1963 by T. S. Eliot, reprinted by permission of the publisher.

Manufactured in the United States of America

For Jim Adams

Contents

Acknowledgments

$\mathcal{T}$his book is dedicated to Jim Adams, rector of St. Mark's Church from 1966 until his retirement in 1996. He led, shaped, and nurtured the place that has been a true community to me for the past fifteen years. Jim encouraged me in this book project and was a regular member of the informal review group that met every couple of months at St. Mark's to discuss my chapter drafts. I am grateful as well to the other members of that group: Linda Barnes, Karen Byrne, Ann Craig, Linda Ewald, and John Lineberger. They were a valuable source of information, criticism, laughter, and support, and they rescued me from many errors. The remaining errors are, of course, my responsibility.

My thanks to the many people at St. Mark's and elsewhere who granted me interviews for this book. Thanks also to those who took the time to provide thoughtful responses to my questionnaire about their religious beliefs. Finally, I am indebted to my agent, Jane Dystel, and to Karen Reeds and Martha Heller, my editors at Rutgers University Press.

Preface

$\mathcal{T}$his book is about my experience as a skeptical member of St. Mark's, an Episcopal church located on Capitol Hill in Washington, D.C. I was raised a Roman Catholic, left that Church during college after I stopped believing in God or in any religious doctrine, and stayed away from churches for the next twenty-five years. I first went to St. Mark's in 1982 at a low point in my life, attracted by the thoughtful, questioning approach to religious issues, by the diverse and vital community, and, to my surprise, by the traditional liturgy—the words and the music. I've been an active member of St. Mark's for fifteen years, including stints as editor of the newsletter, elected member of the Vestry (the governing body), and Sunday school teacher.

This isn't another book about a former skeptic who rediscovers religious belief in middle age as the shadows begin to lengthen. The shelves are heavy with books about personal journeys from faith, to agnosticism, to an epiphany, and back to faith. I didn't believe in God when I came to St. Mark's and I still don't. Most members of St. Mark's are believers—it is a house of God—but I've always been open about where I stand and accepted for what I am. This book is unique for its description of what some churches can offer skeptical people without requiring them to sacrifice their intellectual integrity.

Many Protestant churches have a typical profile: old, white, rigidly doctrinaire, and sexist. These churches are closed in every sense, and they are losing members every year. Some liberal Protestant churches in urban areas are growing by reaching out to young people, blacks and Hispanics, gays and lesbians, agnostics and atheists. Greater vitality in community life and sensitivity to feminist concerns usually accompany a diverse membership, which, in turn, may lead to more democratic ways of running the church. When these elements coalesce, they form what I call an "open church"—the kind of church a skeptic might be interested in.

Being openly skeptical in a Christian church is the book's major theme.

I found I could join in the Lord's Prayer—even though there is no "Father in Heaven" for me—as a powerful metaphor for yearnings felt by skeptics and believers alike, and as a link to a rich tradition going back two thousand years.

Chapters that relate indirectly to the skeptic theme (chapter 12, "Women at St. Mark's"; chapter 13, "Gays and Lesbians at St. Mark's") are nevertheless relevant because an open church like St. Mark's welcomes and extends equal opportunities to everyone in the community. Conversely, if a congregation has a sexist mentality, as many do, it's unlikely to extend a genuine welcome to such minorities as blacks, gays, skeptics.

Several chapters provide examples of what community life can be like in an open church—warts and all. After the first year, I didn't spend much time pondering abstract questions about God. Once I was satisfied that a skeptic could be comfortable in the Episcopal Church—it has no doctrines one must believe on pain of expulsion—it was time to move on. There's a church to run (chapter 9, "Who's in Charge Here?") or a class of third graders to teach (chapter 11, "Christian Education Teacher"). For some, there will be a separation and divorce to suffer through. The reaction of many at St. Mark's to my divorce (chapter 17) was so disappointing to me that I considered leaving for another church.

A word about terminology. I'm an agnostic who finds the evidence of a deity unpersuasive. I use the broader word "skeptic" to describe my philosophical orientation because, beyond agnosticism, it implies a questioning approach to all religious issues. Although I'm not a believer, I spell "God" with the initial capital out of respect for those who are.

The book covers the period January 1982, when I came to St. Mark's, until July 1996, when I returned from a trip to Honduras with a church group (chapter 16, "My Brother's Keeper"). The book's end coincides with the retirement of Rector Jim Adams and the beginning of the search for a new rector—an elaborate and protracted process involving an interim rector, a search committee, the Vestry, many congregational meetings, and some anxiety about the future character of the church Jim did so much to mold.

I expect the search to be successful, that St. Mark's will continue as an open and vital church, while growing in some new directions. But if that doesn't happen, I'm not bound to St. Mark's or to the Episcopal Church with hoops of steel. I could look for another open church and, in Washington, D.C., I'm sure I'd find one.

J.L.K.
Takoma Park, Maryland
September 1996

Skeptic in the House of God

Chapter 1

Skeptic on the Edge

All of us are lost, and know it, and we simply try to settle into our lostness as comfortably and with as much good manners and little curiosity as we can.
—Richard Ford, *The Sportswriter*

"Well Jim, are you going to become an Episcopalian?" Anne Amy, an Episcopal priest, asked the big question as she sat down beside me late that Saturday night in Rehoboth, Delaware, a few blocks from the Atlantic Ocean. I was there as a member of a confirmation class from St. Mark's, an Episcopal church in Washington, D.C. Anne was one of our teachers. About twenty of us had driven there in January for a weekend retreat, the idea being that the deserted beaches and leaden waves would foster contemplation. Sitting by the fireplace during the social hour, I was contemplating a Rolling Rock and wondering, once more, what I was doing there.

I knew what had attracted me to St. Mark's the year before. My professional life was stagnant, I had few friends, and I was suffering from recurrent depressions that were not responding to medication or psychotherapy. St. Mark's, with its reputation as a friendly, vibrant community, represented a lifeline. And after I had begun to attend services, I was surprised to find myself moved by prayers and hymns similar to those I had grown up with as a Catholic.

But I had a problem. I didn't believe in God. Or in an afterlife. Or, for that matter, in any of the traditional doctrines of Christianity. Could I become a member of a church that worships Christ as the Son of God without compromising my intellectual integrity? Could I say the prayers and sing the hymns yet remain an honest skeptic? Could I express my skepticism openly, or would there be pressure to keep it in the closet? I knew I couldn't live with that.

Part of me wanted to answer yes to Anne's question. The thought of leaving my St. Mark's friends was depressing. I would miss reciting the Lord's Prayer and singing "O God Our Help in Ages Past" on Sunday morning. But my intellect was still pulling me in the other direction. I paused and replied, "I don't know yet."

Up to that point, I had felt like a visitor at St. Mark's. I hadn't been asked to make affirmations of faith or commitments of any kind. I kept my distance in other ways—not going to the altar for the bread and wine, not getting down on my knees for the ritual Confession of Sin. But I felt that my visitor's visa was about to expire. I had to make a decision.

A skeptical person's returning to church in middle age is often associated with a crisis—divorce, death in the family—the kind of crisis that might send others into therapy. But when I started going to St. Mark's in 1982, twenty-five years after leaving the Catholic Church, there was no visible crisis. On the surface at least, my life seemed satisfying and predictable, if not exactly serene.

I was forty-seven, educated, employed, married, the father of two bright and healthy children, owner of a home, a car, and a dog. I appeared to be a mainstream kind of guy, someone to be envied.

I had B.A. and law degrees from the University of Iowa, and had been working as a lawyer for twenty years—beginning with a prestigious Wall Street firm, moving to the Civil Rights Division of the U.S. Department of Justice in the mid-1960s, and to nuclear power regulation in the 1970s. During the early 1980s, I was an administrative judge for the U.S. Nuclear Regulatory Commission, responsible for holding public hearings on licenses to operate commercial nuclear power plants. My office was within walking distance from my home, I wasn't overworked, and I was making about $65,000 per year, plus fringe benefits—not great, but not bad.

I had met my wife at a garden party in Georgetown seventeen years earlier. Neither she nor I then had any connection with a church, and religion wasn't even a topic of conversation between us. We were married six months later in a private home by a judge for whom I had worked in the Justice Department. The judge and I wore business suits. Somebody put a Bach partita on the record player. Nobody prayed. Both sets of parents attended, concealing any regrets they might have felt about the relentlessly civil ceremony.

We settled in the Washington area and, after our son and daughter were born, bought our first house—a brick Colonial—in the District. The kids grew up attractive and bright. They did their homework and set the table without being told more than twice. We thought swearing was a healthy form of expression, and the kids learned from us. It never occurred to us to have them baptized. By the time I began agonizing over Episcopal confirmation in 1982, the kids were in their teens—too old to be led off to Sunday school.

Our second house in Chevy Chase, Maryland, was a stately, two-story Tudor—lots of windows, high ceilings with crown molding, and fireplaces in the living room and master bedroom. The house had been in disrepair when we bought it for $152,000 in 1978. I reroofed the garage, mopped water out of the basement when it rained hard, and built a deck in the back. We made do with window units, diverting the $10,000 cost of central air-conditioning to pay college tuition.

The family car was a used 1979 Ford Fairmont station wagon with a heavy body and a small engine. It did not drive, so much as lumber down the street. Something was always wrong with the Ford, usually the brakes. But it got my wife where she wanted to go, got my daughter to her dance classes, and submitted to the kids' driving lessons. I was content, for then, to put my Porsche fantasy on my deferred gratification list.

The family dog was a mutt named Charlie who had come to us as a puppy. Charlie's mother was a basset hound, his father a German shepherd. This bizarre combination gave Charlie a head too small for his body (rather like the Ford Fairmont), and he was, overall, kind of funny looking. But Charlie was very friendly—the only dog I ever knew who could smile. Charlie used to jog around the neighborhood with me before his hips started to give out.

These were some of the observable facts of my life in 1982 when I first went to St. Mark's, the way I imagine the neighbors would have seen me. But beneath that stable, conventional surface, I felt frustrated, isolated, and sometimes depressed.

I was heavily invested in being a lawyer. I was my work. My job as a judge for the Nuclear Regulatory Commission often left me with the feeling that I didn't make a difference—a common and corrosive feeling, especially in government work. The hearings I presided over were honest, and there was the possibility that opponents of a nuclear plant might prevent it from being licensed, at least temporarily. But the hearings were only one part of the licensing process, a part the Commission could, and sometimes did, overrule. There was a widespread feeling that the Commission had a pro-industry bias, and that the hearings were window dressing.

There were other things I didn't like about my job. I was one of about twenty judges hired over the years under varying standards. Perhaps half of my colleagues were well qualified and did a day's work for a day's pay. A few others were at least minimally qualified, with varying degrees of dedication. The rest were incompetent, lazy, or both. Yet we were all paid the same salary. Nobody ever got fired, or even criticized, for substandard work or lack of effort. I was part of a system that rewarded mediocrity.

From time to time, I thought about my former colleagues on the *Iowa Law Review*. One had become a federal judge. Another was the general counsel of a Fortune 500 company. A third was a partner in a prestigious firm in Chicago. At forty-seven, I would have had a hard time getting a better job, and I had two kids to put through college. I felt trapped. Worse than that, I had not lived up to expectations—my own and others'.

My wife and I married only once, but it seemed that we went through several marriages before we separated in 1991, after twenty-five years together. In 1982, when this story begins, we had been struggling for some time to make our marriage work. At one low point, we had joined a group of married couples that met with a psychotherapist every Thursday from 7:30 to 9:00 a.m. The sessions were usually spirited, supportive, and often angry. We surfaced a lot of typical marital issues: sex, money, alcohol, child rearing, and unhealthy interactions with one another.

We stayed in the couples group for four years as our marriage improved. We went to London together and made a ski trip to Austria. My job as deputy general counsel of the Nuclear Regulatory Commission was satisfying. My wife was finishing up a graduate degree and working part-time in her new field after a decade as a full-time mother.

By 1982, however, our marriage became troubled once more. Dissatisfaction with my job was part of the problem. My father died. We had not been close—quite the opposite—but his death nevertheless affected me. I was having periodic problems with depression. I would drink two or three glasses of wine with supper, often followed by one or two beers before bedtime. Most evenings, I settled down in front of the television—emotionally and intellectually unavailable. Of course, drinking made the depression worse.

I felt isolated from life outside my family. I was born in a small Iowa farm town where everybody knows everybody else. Chevy Chase, Maryland, is a prestigious address, but for me it was an anonymous, sterile place to live. Over the years, my wife and I developed casual acquaintances with a few other couples on the block, but our lives ran on different tracks. The reclusive widow next door was better off left alone. When my wife and I separated, our neighbors—apparently fearing separations might be contagious—backed away even farther. When we sold the family home in Chevy Chase after fourteen years I said good-bye to two people.

As I was to learn later, an active church congregation can provide the strong sense of community so often lacking in urban life. Religion was seldom discussed among our middle-class friends and neighbors in Washington; most of them had no church affiliation and few, if any, religious practices. Our Jewish friends held bar and bat mitzvahs for their sons and daughters, but those were as much social as religious occasions. The few people we knew who did go to church regularly, mostly Catholics, we regarded rather patronizingly.

I had two close male friends, one of whom was living in the Philippines. My other friend had spent two years with me in a therapy group in the mid-1970s, so we were accustomed to talking at a personal level. But one real friend wasn't enough. My other male acquaintances were limited by the unspoken assumption that personal matters are to be kept that way. When we talked, we talked about politics, the Redskins, our children, or the weather. I never knew what was going on inside the other guy, or he in me.

So there I was in the winter of 1982, keeping up a brave front but sinking inside—a candidate for just about any form of self-improvement, even a church.

My wife and I had heard about St. Mark's from friends who spoke of it enthusiastically. The congregation was full of friendly people with varied backgrounds. Lay members helped plan the services, even shaping sermons and picking the hymns. While that all sounded interesting, much of it novel, the idea of a confirmed skeptic like me going to a Christian church seemed like selling out. How could I square my intellectual convictions with the central purpose of the church: to worship a God I didn't believe in?

Chapter 2

First Sunday

Teach us to care and not to care
Teach us to sit still.

—T. S. Eliot, "Ash Wednesday"

One Sunday morning in January 1982, my wife and I drove the twelve miles from Chevy Chase to St. Mark's Church in the District of Columbia. I didn't go because of our friends' glowing descriptions or because I had worked out an intellectually respectable rebuttal to my skepticism—I hadn't. I wasn't conscious of voids in my life that a church might fill. And I don't think I would have gone by myself. I went because my wife was going, because my curiosity had been aroused, and because I didn't want to miss out on something interesting.

We found St. Mark's on Capitol Hill, just behind the Library of Congress. The building's architecture is an unusual mixture of Gothic and Romanesque. With its aged red brick, slate roof, tall steeple, and stained-glass windows, it looked the way I thought a church ought to look. According to a plaque near one entrance, the cornerstone had been laid in 1888 and the building was listed in the National Register of Historic Places. I had the fleeting thought that if God were to be found anywhere in Washington, D.C.—which I very much doubted—this was as likely a place as any.

I remember standing on the sidewalk outside, simultaneously attracted and repelled, and wondering what I was doing there. Then we walked through massive wooden doors into the church. Arriving well before the start of the service, we didn't see any of our friends, so we took seats and waited. I was aware of mixed feelings. I felt superior, probably the only rational person on the premises. I felt isolated, a trespasser on consecrated ground. I also felt defensive. Perhaps I should carry a sign—"skeptical ex-Catholic"—like a leper's bell. At the same time, I imagined that the assembled faithful could see right through me and know I didn't belong there.

The congregation that Sunday morning was made up of men and women in about equal numbers; most appeared to be between the ages of thirty and sixty. There were a few older people, but I didn't notice any fur coats or blue hair—hallmarks of many aging Protestant congregations. Although Capitol Hill is a racially mixed neighborhood, the congregation of about two hundred that morning was white, except for three or four blacks. I found that puzzling. I learned later that most of the children and many of the younger people had attended a nine o'clock service in which the liturgy and ambience are less formal, with a seminar format for the sermon, something in the liturgy for the kids, and folk music with guitars. We had come to the more formal service at eleven, with a lecture-type sermon, organ music, and other traditional trappings.

Some in the congregation that morning were formally dressed (coats and ties, dresses, a few churchy-looking hats), but most came informally (faded jeans, baggy sweaters, worn sneakers). In spite of the tacky attire, these people had the unmistakable look of middle-class professionals. This was my first hint of what was meant by the phrase "tacky chic" at St. Mark's. My next indication would come from the men's restroom—an ancient, grungy, one-stall cubicle where I was to rub elbows with a lot of people after coffee. Tacky chic was part of St. Mark's charm through the 1980s. The $2 million renovation of 1991 included new restrooms, but the dress code remained unchanged.

I had always thought of churches as having pews—places for the congregation to sit a respectful distance from the celebrants of the service. Stationary pews send a confining message: sit down and be quiet. The pews at St. Mark's had been replaced with movable chairs so that services could be conducted in the round, closer to the congregation. The nave—the biggest space in the church—was open to movement and conversation before the service began. And with the pews gone, the exposed rafters peaking high above the original pine floor magnified the sensation of open space.

On that first Sunday, a pewless church struck an old Catholic like me as an innovation. Later on, Jim Adams, the rector of St. Mark's and a church history buff, set me straight about churches and pews. According to Adams, prior to Oliver Cromwell's Protectorate and the ascendancy of Puritanism in seventeenth-century England, churches didn't have pews. It was the custom to gather and socialize in the churches on holidays, when the church wardens would roll out a barrel of beer on the open church floor. Pews—along with destruction of stained glass and organ removal—were Puritan responses to loose behavior. Viewed in historical perspective, the removal of the pews at St. Mark's in the 1960s rebuked a Puritan innovation and reinstated a church tradition.

I paused to admire the breathtakingly beautiful stained glass in the windows of the church. I was to learn that most of it was made by Mayer of Munich, a leading German manufacturer of stained glass since 1845. The front window, "Christ Leaving the Praetorium," dominates the nave; it was made in 1888 by the studio of Louis Comfort Tiffany, source of some of the finest stained glass of that period.

Before the service started, most in the congregation were engaged in animated conversations—a few sitting, others standing in the aisles or leaning against the walls—just about everywhere but seated on the altar. It was a lively, disorderly scene, quite unlike the muffled murmurings I had grown up with in the pews of Catholic churches. Judging from demeanor and snatches of overheard conversation, I got the impression that these were intelligent people—challenging my long-held contrary belief about church-goers.

Still waiting for the service to get under way, I thumbed through *The Book of Common Prayer*—first compiled by Archbishop Cramner in 1549 during the reign of Henry VIII. As I recalled, Henry had broken with Rome— freeing the Church of England from papal control—not out of religious conviction but to pave the way for his divorce from his first wife, Catherine of Aragon. He had later gotten rid of his second and fifth wives, Anne Boleyn and Katherine Howard, by having them beheaded. A sinner myself, I felt more at home thinking that St. Mark's traced its origins to a world-class sinner like Henry.

The Book of Common Prayer is replete with references to God and includes the "Thirty-nine Articles"—a list of theological propositions developed by English bishops in 1562 and adopted by the American Episcopal Convention of 1801 for the guidance of the faithful. Article IV, for example, states that Christ "did truly rise again from death, and took again his body. . . wherewith he ascended into Heaven." Skimming the Articles, I didn't think I could buy any of them, and it began to look as if I would be out of this church in short order. But I hadn't been asked to affirm my belief in the Articles, at least not yet. Sufficient unto the day is the evil thereof, I thought, recalling one of the few passages I knew from the Bible (Matthew 6:34).

The service got under way with a hymn and a procession to the altar by priests (as Episcopal clergy are called), acolytes (the equivalent of Catholic Mass servers), and several laypeople who would assist in distributing the bread and wine at "the Eucharist" (similar to the Catholic Communion). The service was conducted jointly by two priests—a man and a woman. The woman priest was quite obviously in the advanced stages of pregnancy. As an ex-Catholic, I was accustomed to male priests being in charge of everything. I was impressed.

As the service progressed, I realized that the Episcopal Sunday liturgy is similar in many ways to a Catholic Mass. There are hymns, prayers, readings of an Epistle and a Gospel, and a sermon. The Nicene Creed ("I believe in one God, the Father Almighty, Maker of Heaven and Earth . . . ") and the Lord's Prayer are recited by the congregation and are virtually identical to their Catholic counterparts, except that Episcopalians add a rhetorical flourish ("for thine is the kingdom, the power, and the glory") at the end of the Lord's Prayer.

I had conflicted feelings when we came to the Nicene Creed. Yet there was something strangely compelling about this ancient declaration of faith I had known all my life, as it was recited by the congregation in that lovely old church on a winter Sunday morning. I stood silent and perplexed. It would be some time before I could approach the Nicene Creed historically and symbolically.

I was put off by another prayer carried over from the Catholic liturgy—the Confession of Sin. I sat in pained silence while the members of the congregation got down on their knees (kneelers for the dignified, the cold floor for the truly penitent) and confessed, in nonspecific unison, their "manifold sins and wickedness, in thought, word and deed." This struck me as medieval and downright degrading. I wasn't going to get down on my knees for anybody. After the Confession of Sin was recited, the rector rose and forgave everybody their sins, en masse. Recalling those excruciating times when I had to tell a Catholic priest, one on one, the specifics of my sins of the flesh, I thought to myself: these people are getting off easy.

Ironically, after fifteen years at St. Mark's the Confession of Sin has become one of the most important parts of the service to me. I like to get down on my knees on that old wooden floor and think about what I've done wrong, where I've fallen short. Confession is good for the soul (or one's psychological well-being), even without God or a confessional box.

Rector Adams delivered the sermon that morning. I don't remember what he said or even what it was about. Two things did stick in my mind.

Adams spoke in concrete terms about life in the real world—unlike the abstract, theological discourses I had heard from Catholic priests years ago. And it was obvious to me that Adams was an intelligent guy. I couldn't imagine that he really believed in the virgin birth or the bodily resurrection of the dead. Maybe there was some way to make sense out of this place, after all.

About halfway through the service, there was a break while the collection plate was passed and announcements were made. The break disrupted the flow of the service. At the same time, it seemed to provide a relief after a prolonged period of solemnity and before the most solemn part of the service, the Holy Eucharist. It's hard to sit still for so long on Sunday morning when you're not used to it.

I put a couple of dollars in the plate—that seemed about right for a skeptical visitor—without pausing to compare my offering to the cost of a movie ticket. Most people didn't put anything in the plate, and I wondered how this church paid its bills. What I didn't know was that members make annual pledges (a lot more than two dollars a week), and some pay their pledges in a lump sum.

I had always thought of churches as places people go for an hour on Sunday morning. The announcements—a minor art form at St. Mark's— changed my perspective. Eight or ten people mounted the pulpit in turn, introduced themselves, and made pitches for everything from a food-for-the-homeless program, to the St. Mark's Players' latest production, to an assortment of committee activities—including something called the Committee to Have More Fun. I began to realize that the Sunday service was only one part of what went on at St. Mark's, and that this was a community of extraordinary diversity and vitality.

After the announcements, the formal service resumed, culminating in the Eucharist—the blessing and distribution of bread and wine to the congregation. The Episcopal Eucharist and the Catholic Communion, the liturgical heart of both services, are similar in form but quite different in theological significance. Catholics believe in "transubstantiation": when the bread and wine are consecrated—while remaining unchanged in appearance—they become the literal body and blood of Christ, which may be received only by Catholics in a state of grace. As a kid, I had been taught that if a Catholic were to take Communion while in the state of mortal sin (my customary state), his sins would be compounded.

In an Episcopal service, the bread and wine are considered symbolic of the body and blood of Christ, but not the real thing—a concept skeptics like me find easier to accept. Everyone in the congregation is invited to receive the Eucharist, including visitors, unrepentant sinners, and street people (if any are in attendance that morning).

Whatever else may be said about the two services, an Episcopal Eucharist tastes better than a Catholic Communion. Catholics get a small, dry wafer that sticks to the roof of your mouth, and no wine. In Episcopal churches, communion is celebrated with wine and either wafers or real bread. At St. Mark's, the bread and wine are contributed by parishioners. Contributions are duly noted in the Sunday *Bulletin*, lending a competitive edge to an act of charity. Typically, St. Mark's bread is a great golden globe from a bakery; sometimes it's home baked; Wonder Bread is out. Wine contributions vary, from seven-dollar-a-liter California red to medium-grade French. Easter, the most festive day of the church year, is celebrated with champagne; the clergy pop the corks, which fly in graceful parabolas from the altar into the congregation.

We came to the Lord's Prayer just before the bread and wine were distributed. To my surprise, I found myself suspending my intellectual censors and joining in the recitation. Unlike the Nicene Creed, the Lord's Prayer is simple, direct, and compelling:

> Give us this day our daily bread,
> and forgive us our trespasses,
> as we forgive those who trespass against us.

The words express universal thoughts and yearnings, whether addressed to a "Father in Heaven" or not. When the Lord's Prayer was over, I was confused. Here I was, reciting a prayer to a God I didn't believe in. Yet I felt the spirit of the prayer was profoundly true, and there was a powerful sense of community in reciting it with others.

That first morning at St. Mark's, I didn't accept the rector's invitation to communion—as he put it, "to share the bread and wine at the Lord's table." Communion seemed to represent the very thing I had rejected so many years ago. I felt okay sitting in as a skeptical observer—like Margaret Mead observing the Samoans—but I wasn't about to participate in the most solemn part of the service. At least not yet.

There is such a thing as a free lunch if you're a first-time visitor at St. Mark's. My wife and I were invited after the service to lunch in "the Pub," which, we were told, was in the basement. We wound our way down battered, unsafe-looking stairs and into a dank basement room (more tacky chic), identifiable as the Pub because someone in a T-shirt was dispensing beer from a tap. A bar in a church. What kind of church was this?

Someone gave us a beer and pointed us toward the "Pub Lunch" table. People were friendly and seemed genuinely interested in us. The service over, there was no more talk of God, which I found a relief. The food wasn't bad. We felt welcome to come back, but it was all very low-key.

In the days following that first morning at St. Mark's, the idea of joining such a friendly and active community seemed like a real possibility. I was surprised at how strongly and positively the ex-Catholic in me had responded to parts of the service. But when I thought back on my experience as a young Catholic, most of my recollections were distasteful, some of them painful. In any case, I didn't entirely trust my emotional reactions, and my intellectual skepticism was unshaken, as it would remain. My skeptical feelings and opinions run deep, and for good reason.

Chapter 3

A Good Catholic Boy Goes Wrong

"Well, now that we have seen each other," said the Unicorn, "if you believe in me, I'll believe in you. Is that a bargain?"
—Lewis Carroll, *Through the Looking Glass.*

I got religion as a boy from my Irish Catholic father's side. He was born on a farm in Allamakee County, Iowa, an area settled by immigrant Irish farmers. One of his uncles was a priest, one of his aunts a nun. Partly because of the Church's ban on birth control but also to put more hands in the field, my father's kinfolk had large families; ten or twelve children were common. Some of them were named after a pope or obscure saint, like my father's cousins Urban Kelley and Cleophus Heffern. Except when the roads were impassable—rural blacktops were the exception around World War I—the Kelley family went to Mass every Sunday morning at Cherry Mound Church, a white frame structure surrounded by cornfields. My father remained a devout Catholic all his life. I don't think it ever occurred to him to question his faith.

My father hated farming. He escaped by working his way through the University of Iowa dental school. After graduating in 1929, he opened a one-flight-up dental practice in Harlan, the county seat of Shelby County in southwestern Iowa, population 4,500, where he met and courted my mother, a schoolteacher.

Shelby County was settled by immigrant Danish Protestants. My maternal grandfather, Louis Christensen, was a blacksmith who came over in steerage at nineteen to avoid the Danish draft. My mother was raised a Lutheran, but she had a skeptical turn of mind and was indifferent to religious doctrine. When she married my father, she agreed to convert to Catholicism and to have the children raised in the Catholic faith.

I was born in my grandfather's house in Harlan in 1935. The state's farm economy hadn't yet recovered from the depression, and it was cheaper to have a baby delivered at home. I lived with my parents in my grandfather's house until age six, when the war started and my father, an army reservist, was called to active duty.

My life as a Catholic began when I was taken to St. Cecelia's Church in Harlan to be baptized. Father Callahan poured holy water on my head and said the ritual words. With baptism behind me, I was not bothered much with religion until I reached school age.

In the early 1940s my father was transferred to Arkansas in the wartime army. I attended Immaculate Conception, a Catholic school taught by nuns in Fort Smith. We had religion class every day. The nuns taught us that Jesus had been conceived in Mary's womb by a visitation from the Holy Ghost—a miraculous exception to the laws of nature called the "virgin birth." We were also taught that the pope was infallible "in matters of faith and morals." This meant that if the pope declared something to be so—such as the virgin birth—it *was* so, regardless of any evidence to the contrary. I was eight years old and accepted the nuns' teachings without question.

One Sunday morning when I was about ten I had my first really unpleasant experience with the Catholic Church—perhaps a seed of my later defection. Our family had gone to church in Leesville, Louisiana, near Fort Polk where my father was then stationed, and the priest announced that he needed someone to serve Mass.

Servers of Mass are called "altar boys" (girls weren't allowed to serve). They wear a black robe, called a "cassock," and a loose-fitting, shirtlike garment, called a "surplice." Servers assist the priest by responding in Latin to prescribed prayers, by handing him cruets (little bottles) of wine and water, and by ringing a bell when the Communion wafers and wine are being consecrated—transformed into the body and blood of Christ. The wafers are distributed to the congregation at Holy Communion. The acolyte trails the priest and holds a plate under the recipient's chin to catch any stray crumbs of the consecrated wafer.

That Sunday morning in Leesville, my father, the good Catholic parent, saw it as his duty to respond to the priest's request for assistance. With a muttered "Get up there," he pushed me out of our pew and up the aisle, an about-to-be-burnt offering. I didn't know a word of Latin, had no idea what I was supposed to do, and was terrified at the thought of stumbling around in a dress in front of all those people.

The priest and I walked to the altar, and he motioned to me where to kneel. I knelt, and he delivered his opening line: *Introibo ad altarem Dei* ("I will go unto the altar of God"). I was supposed to respond: *Ad Deum qui laetificat juventutem meam* ("To God who gives joy to my youth")—a mouthful for any ten-year-old. The priest's lines and my responses were printed on a plastic card, but I couldn't read the Latin, and I was too scared to say anything, even if I could. The priest mumbled something to cover me, and we pressed on.

I didn't know when or where to sit, stand, or kneel. I couldn't find the wine and water. After the priest showed me, I spilled the wine on the carpeting. As he held the king-size, ceremonial wafer aloft in consecration, I couldn't get the bell to ring (the clapper had somehow gotten stuck). Finally, Mass was over, and I stumbled away from the altar behind the priest, tripping on my cassock. The priest seemed glad to see me leave.

Despite that and other misadventures, I remained a serious Catholic until I left the Church at twenty-one—more serious, it seemed to me, than most others my age. Looking back on it, I would have been better off if I hadn't taken the Church and its teachings so much to heart, particularly when it came to sex.

The Catholic Church has a lot to say about sex. Its thinkers and spokesmen are popes, cardinals, bishops and priests—all of whom have taken a vow of celibacy. But that doesn't deter them from pontificating on the subject. According to the Catholic Church, the only legitimate purpose of sex is procreation. Sex as an expression of love, or merely to satisfy sexual desire—lust, if you will—is sinful. Sex with a birth control device is a sin. So is masturbation.

Even *thinking* about sex can be a sin, making movies and television "occasions of sin" (Catholic terminology) on a massive scale. When the sap was first rising in my generation, our sexual fantasies were fed by Jane Russell's cleavage in *The Outlaw* and by Marilyn Monroe, top to bottom, in *Some Like It Hot*. Nowadays, of course, media invitations to sex are more explicit.

But there is hope for the conscientious Catholic cast adrift in this sea of sensuality. The Church draws a fine, but saving, distinction where "impure thoughts" are concerned. An impure thought can enter your mind, so to speak, against your will—for example, when you channel surf to an old Marilyn Monroe movie just as she is crossing her legs. If you immediately dismiss Ms. Monroe from your mind without mentally unzipping your pants, you haven't sinned. It's only when you "entertain" the fantasy that you get into trouble. When an impure thought intrudes, unwanted, into your consciousness, a priest might recommend that you switch your attention to something nonsexual—such as an uplifting scene from nature or your bank balance. Better yet, say "Hail Marys" until the fantasy passes.

During the 1960s, Philip Roth's novel *Portnoy's Complaint* made public the seldom-discussed fact that teenage boys masturbate a lot. I was sure I was headed straight to Hell, but for years I was too embarrassed to confess my sins of the flesh. Finally, Father Clasby—a genial Irish priest for whom I served Mass when my father was stationed at an army base in Alaska—took it upon himself to channel my sexual development from behind his confessional screen, extracting the sordid facts from me like so many impacted molars. He hammered away with questions about sex until I cracked, and my depravity poured out like excrement, metaphorically spattering the walls and fouling the floor of the confessional. When he had heard it all, he murmured the Latin words of absolution (*Ego te absolvo*) and told me, "Go and sin no more."

But I was weak. Within a day or two I fell back into sin, followed by more confessions, more absolutions, and more sexual indulgence—an endless cycle of sin, repentance, and more sin. I felt doomed and alone. Looking back, I know I had a lot of company—virtually every teenage boy in the world. But we Catholic boys knew enough to be ashamed, and we kept our self-abuses to ourselves.

All of this might not have been so bad except for the psychological damage done to those of us who took it seriously. The Catholic Church made me think of sex as an evil, instead of one of the wonders of life. I spent a lot of time in psychotherapy later on, undoing the damage.

My family continued to follow my father in his military assignments, and I spent my junior year in a Jesuit high school in Washington, D.C. Named for St. Aloysius Gonzaga, a sixteenth-century patron of education, Gonzaga High School was an excellent place to learn Latin, Greek, and trigonometry. There was, of course, a regular class in religion, and attendance at Friday morning Mass was mandatory. I also learned that religious instruction can be indirect. Only Catholic poets were represented in our English literature class. Literary standards were sometimes maintained— for example, with Gerard Manley Hopkins's "Pied Beauty." But I had to admire our teacher, a young Jesuit with iron self-control, when he managed to discourse on Joyce Kilmer's "Trees" without cracking a smile.

After my father retired from the military, my family moved back to Iowa, and I finished high school there in 1953. Although I fell in with some questionable companions—we drank Budweiser, smoked Camels, and gambled away our grocery clerk earnings—I was still a Catholic in good standing.

My freshman year at the University of Iowa posed no danger to my faith. I served Mass most Sundays for Father Welch at the Newman Club Chapel. At first, I continued to say my prayers on my knees before going to bed, but few of my fraternity brothers at the SAE house did likewise. As a freshman wishing to conform in all things, I started saying my prayers in bed.

Most of the required courses in the freshman year were long on skill development and short on intellectual content. The survey course on Western civilization did bring out some of the historic excesses of the Church—the sale of indulgences and the dalliances of Renaissance popes—which had led to the Reformation. But Catholics are practiced in distinguishing the failings of individuals from the infallibility of the Church.

The real trouble started in my sophomore year, when I took a course called "Introduction to Modern Philosophy." We read Descartes, Hobbes, Hume, and Berkeley. Forty years later, I don't remember their arguments in detail. I do remember the skepticism with which they approached things most people take for granted, a spirit captured in Descartes's famous dictum: *Cogito, ergo sum* ("I think, therefore I am"). This dictum had numerous variations, intellectual and profane, including my favorite graffiti over the urinal at Kenny's Bar and Grill in Iowa City: *Urinato, ergo sum.*

I was attracted to the philosophy of determinism. As determinists like Hobbes and Hume saw it, everything in the universe, including human behavior, is determined by unvarying natural laws. All the things that happen—not only the time and place of physical events, like sunsets and earthquakes, but also human actions and feelings, such as when one eats breakfast or falls in love—can only happen when, where, and in exactly the way they do. It is as if the universe were a giant pool table with billions of balls rolling and colliding in precisely predictable paths, from the beginning to the end of time.

By my junior year in college, I thought determinism was the view of the world that made the most sense to me. But how could a good Catholic embrace a philosophy totally at odds with the concept of free will, a concept central to Catholic doctrine? According to the Church, people are free to choose between good and evil, and if they choose sin and end up in Hell, it's nobody's fault but their own.

Freedom of choice, as Catholics conceive of it, is related to the so-called problem of evil, which has been keeping theologians occupied for centuries. The presence of evil in the world is felt most keenly in the suffering of the innocent. The Holocaust is an extreme example. In a nutshell, the problem is this: If God is all powerful, all good, and all knowing, how can there be evil in the world? Why doesn't God prevent it? Some Catholic theologians like to talk about original sin and the resulting debased natures of people who are endowed with free will. Other theologians have suggested that God has only limited powers, or that He is dead.

Of course, there is evil in the world—too much of it. But if one takes a deterministic view, evil is not a "problem" in the sense that there is an intellectual difficulty in accounting for its presence. Under that view, everything happens for a good and sufficient reason, just as it *has* to happen. Innocent people die in earthquakes and jetliner crashes not because God has been callous or negligent, but because the ongoing momentum of the universe put them in the wrong place at the wrong time.

I spent a lot of time walking around the campus in Iowa City as a sophomore and junior struggling to reconcile Catholic teachings on free will and the problem of evil with my growing belief in determinism, while my fraternity brothers were out drinking beer or trying to get laid. I failed.

I don't understand modern physics or quantum mechanics. My last attempt was Stephen Hawking's *A Brief History of Time.* He lost me on page thirteen. I mention this because some physicists—Niels Bohr, for one—and so-called postmodernist theologians have cited evidence of indeterminacy of matter at the subatomic level to support philosophical and theological arguments for free will. Despite the opinion of Hawking and others that subatomic particles don't behave lawfully, I still believe that they do, and that those laws will be discovered someday. I'm only a layman, but I have some distinguished company in that belief. Einstein stood for a deterministic view of the world, including its subatomic level, in his famous rejoinder to Bohr: "God does not play dice with the universe." But even if Hawking and Bohr are right, it doesn't seem to me to follow that indeterminacy of subatomic particles somehow transmits free will to the grosser forces that presumably control human behavior.

There were other intellectual influences pushing me away from Catholicism in my college days. I chose an interdisciplinary major in humanities, with an emphasis on philosophy, history, English, and great-books courses. My reading list came to include Camus, Dostoyevsky, Joyce, Kant, Luther, Russell, Santayana, Sartre, Twain, and Voltaire, among others. None of these writers supported the Catholic viewpoint.

I developed a philosophy and, if you will, religion of my own—a personalized version of secular humanism. To me, Dr. Rieux, the protagonist in Camus's *The Plague* who fought to save his patients, was as good a role model as anyone in the Bible. Although I couldn't prove that God doesn't exist, the weight of the evidence appeared to be against it. And even if some Higher Power created the universe, there seemed little reason to believe that he is still around or, even if he were, that he took any interest in me. In any case, I wanted to make my own value judgments. I thought it should be enough if I develop my own gifts and do some good for others from time to time—or at least not do any harm. Nothing in the years since college has caused me to change those basic conclusions.

Summer school in Iowa City in 1956 led to a crisis of faith. One Thursday night toward the end of the term, I finally decided that I no longer believed in Catholicism, and that I would have to leave the Church. The following day, a Friday, I wanted to take some action to seal my decision. In those days, Catholics were not supposed to eat meat on Friday. (At my fraternity house, the Protestants called us "mackerel snappers.") I went to a downtown restaurant and ordered spaghetti with meat sauce. I almost choked on the meat sauce, but I walked out of the restaurant feeling I had made a crossing.

I stopped going to church, and Father Welch eventually noticed my absence from the Newman Club. When I ran into him on the campus, he said, "I need to talk to you." I knew perfectly well what he meant, and agreed to come to the Newman Club the next day. I arrived to find that Father Welch had handed me off to his deputy, a young Dominican priest. I told him I had lost my faith. He sighed and asked if I was praying for guidance. I said no. That ended the discussion and my life as a Catholic. I never went back.

With so much energy invested in intellectual abstractions, I wasn't prepared for the emotional repercussions of leaving the Church. It felt strange not to be in church on Sunday morning. (Now that I've resumed church-going, I'm more faithful about attending Sunday services than the average Episcopalian.) Through my twenties, I couldn't stand the sound of religious music. I remember going to a Christmas concert by the Minneapolis

Symphony in Iowa City when the orchestra began to play Bach's "Jesu, Joy of Man's Desiring." I suddenly felt sick, got up, and walked out.

Despite the strength of my intellectual convictions, I dreaded telling my parents I had left the Church. My father took it hard, but he came to accept my fall from grace, realizing there was nothing he could do about it. My mother's concerns were more social and pragmatic than spiritual. It was okay with her if I didn't believe in God as long as I kept it to myself when I was home from school. I went along with her for a year or so, but it became harder and harder to fake it when accompanying my parents to Mass. I woke up late one Sunday morning to discover that they had gone to church without me. My mother, the strongest influence in my life, had given up.

I was twenty-one in 1956, the summer I left the Catholic Church. I didn't go inside a church for the next twenty-six years, except for weddings, funerals, or as a tourist in the cathedrals of Europe. I didn't miss church, and I wasn't aware of any religious feelings. My first visits to St. Mark's in the winter of 1982 were almost accidental—the result of curiosity rather than conviction. But despite my qualms about the God-talk there, I was gradually getting hooked.

Chapter 4

First Year

The beginning is the most imporant part of the work.
—Plato, *The Republic*

In the year 325, the emperor Constantine called a council of bishops and theologians to resolve doctrinal differences that had arisen among the early Christians. The council met at Nicaea—in what is now modern Turkey—and hammered out a consensus statement of Christian doctrine, which came to be called the "Nicene Creed." Sixteen centuries later, the Creed became my bête noire at St. Mark's Church.

The St. Mark's congregation recites the Nicene Creed in unison every Sunday morning. A litany of traditional Christian beliefs, the Creed affirms that God created Heaven and Earth, that Mary gave birth as a virgin, that Christ rose from his tomb and ascended bodily into Heaven, and that on the last day we, too, will rise from our graves to be judged. As a Catholic altar boy, I had recited the Creed in Latin. I had no difficulty in accepting it then, perhaps because I didn't know what I was saying. As a newcomer at St. Mark's, I found the Creed incredible—I still do. After about a month of attending Sunday services, I signed up for "Introduction to Life at St. Mark's," thinking the course might give me a new perspective on (or a way to live with) the Nicene Creed.

You can go to church every Sunday morning for years and, if that's the extent of your participation, scarcely get involved in the church community. Most community activity takes place outside services—in classes, charitable projects, social gatherings, retreats. The intro class, as it was called, was my first step into the St. Mark's community.

My wife and I drove to St. Mark's six evenings in the spring of 1982 to attend the class, taught by Rector Jim Adams. Then in his late forties, Adams had grown up in Aurora, Nebraska, population 2,419—a fact which predisposed an Iowan like me in his favor. He had subsidized his B.A. degree in political science from George Washington University with a job as an elevator operator in the Senate Office Building. As graduation approached, Adams had no specific plans but began thinking about the ministry, prompted, as he recalls, by advice from his hometown minister's wife: "I had to be either a lawyer or a preacher because of my loud voice."

In those days, there was a clergy shortage in the Episcopal Church. Unlike today, when the glut of candidates permits seminaries to screen and vet for faith, commitment to ministry, and an appropriate personality profile, Adams told me that he wasn't screened at all. "So off I went to seminary, and nobody ever asked me what I believed." Following ordination, he served a stint in an Episcopal mission church in Prince George's County, Maryland, before he was "called" (in church jargon) to St. Mark's in 1966. Jim Adams served as rector of St. Mark's Church for thirty years, until his retirement in 1996.

Jim's manner that first evening of the intro class was friendly and open, if somewhat reserved. He sketched some of his background and told us that he is married, the father of three daughters. He outlined some of the topics we would discuss in the coming weeks: prayer, ritual, death, community, and the Nicene Creed. Apparently I wasn't the only one who had problems with the Creed.

About fifteen newcomers attended the intro class. Much of the first session was devoted to introducing ourselves. We went around the circle, taking turns describing our backgrounds, families, jobs, and what had brought us to St. Mark's. Most of my classmates had been raised in Protestant denominations, but there were several ex-Catholics among us. Those from "mainline" Protestant denominations—Episcopal, Presbyterian, Methodist, Lutheran—appeared to be more or less comfortable with organized religion; some of them spoke (rather cloyingly, I thought) of finding a "new spiritual home" at St. Mark's. I detected a certain unease among us ex-Catholics, as if coming to a Protestant church—the enemy camp—compounded our earlier apostasies. But I may have been projecting my feelings onto them.

I was nervous as my turn approached, wondering whether my skeptical views would be acceptable in that company. What was an agnostic—worse yet, one with strong leanings toward atheism—doing in a church at all? Curiosity didn't seem a sufficient reason. (It was to be several years before tacit acceptance evolved into a declared policy of welcoming skeptics to St. Mark's.) I didn't think I would be asked to leave, but I could imagine an excluding silence falling over the room. I decided not to fudge it. I told the class I was skeptical, an agnostic who hadn't believed in any god since his college days. No one joined me. On the other hand, no one seemed shocked, which was reassuring.

I had signed up for the intro class expecting it to focus on the theology of the Episcopal Church. Coming from a Catholic background, I assumed there was such a thing—an integrated body of religious doctrine to which all Episcopalians were expected to subscribe, on pain of exclusion. If that body of doctrine wasn't the Nicene Creed, then what was it?

As it turned out, I was mistaken on both counts. The class didn't spend much time on theology. And I began to suspect that Episcopalians—at least those at St. Mark's—don't subscribe to any clearly defined body of religious doctrine. As the weeks went by, the church looked more and more like the Democratic Party: a big, shapeless tent under which there was a place for everyone, from traditional believers to skeptics. I was reminded of Will Rogers's remark: "I don't belong to any organized political party. I'm a Democrat."

The intro class focused on human needs and aspirations, how we deal with crises in our lives, how a church can meet our needs and help us through the hard parts. We talked about the church as a community, a place where—to borrow a phrase from a television sitcom—everybody knows your name. We were to discover that St. Mark's is a community to hundreds of people who come together to celebrate their victories, mourn their losses, and support one another in the everyday business of life.

We talked a lot about rituals, particularly those that mark major life passages: baptism, weddings, and funerals. Skeptic that I am, the discussion of baptism gave me a twinge of guilt that my two children had never been baptized. I had rationalized that they could make their own decisions about religion when they grew up. But I also knew that my decision not to expose them to any religious training as children would affect their decisions later on.

Jim Adams wrote a book about the value of churchgoing for skeptics: *So You Think You're Not Religious? A Thinking Person's Guide to the Church*. In his book, Adams cites an incident related by sociologist Milton Kotler about a 1960s wedding that the couple wanted to celebrate without any ritual whatever. They rented a hotel banquet room, set out food and drink, and waited to see what would happen. According to Kotler: "Most of the guests began drinking compulsively, and soon fell into shouting, quarreling, and

weeping. The wedding was like a small-scale riot." Kotler went on to ob-
serve: "Such a disaster was predictable. You can't have a wedding without
ritual. All of the emotions brought to the surface at a wedding must be
channeled or they will overwhelm the gathering. Ritual provides the chan-
nels." This incident reminded me of my 1960s wedding before a judge in a
Georgetown home. Perhaps our exchange of vows and ritual cake cutting
had staved off unruly behavior. In any case, there hadn't been enough guests
for a riot.

"Blessed are those who mourn, for they shall be comforted," Christ
told his followers in the Sermon on the Mount. The intro class devoted a
session to death and the church rituals designed to help the bereaved work
through their grief—an important psychological process that can include
deep and conflicted feelings of loss, anger, and guilt. The reading in *The
Book of Common Prayer* for "The Burial of the Dead" begins with: "I am the
resurrection and the life, saith the Lord. He that believeth in me, though he
were dead, yet shall he live. And whosoever liveth and believeth in me
shall never die."

The Twenty-third Psalm—one of the best-known passages in the
Bible—is another standard reading at Christian funerals. The psalm begins
(in the King James version): "The Lord is my shepherd, I shall not want.
Yea, though I walk through the valley of the shadow of death, I shall fear
no evil." These words can have comforting and healing power, for skeptics
as well as believers, and their poetry is universal.

In his book about skepticism and the church, Jim Adams points out
that the Bible includes at least one skeptical writer. Qoheleth, a Jerusalem
schoolmaster, wrote in the third century before Christ. His work is pre-
served in the Old Testament Book of Ecclesiastes, including this poem:

> For everything its season, and for every activity
> under heaven its time:
> a time to be born and a time to die;
> a time to plant and a time to uproot;
> a time to kill and a time to heal;
> a time to pull down and a time to build up;
> a time to weep and a time to laugh.

This biblical poem was the inspiration for Pete Seeger's song "Turn, Turn,
Turn," popularized by the Byrds in the 1960s.

The topic one evening was private prayer—how to do it and what it can do for you. Jim Adams asked the class about barriers to prayer. I suggested that no one was listening. Others expressed doubt that their prayers would be answered. Reasons enough, I thought, not to pray.

The class brought out some positive reasons to pray, mostly of a psychological nature. Prayer is like meditation, it was said. It helps reduce stress and manage anxiety. But if you're searching for inner peace, I thought, why not take up yoga or transcendental meditation? Others suggested that prayer allows us to focus on what is really important. Maybe so, but it won't get you what you're asking for—it won't cure cancer or bring peace to the Middle East. The discussion was followed by a practice session. We were asked to repeat a mantra: "Lord Jesus Christ, have mercy on me, a sinner." I couldn't force myself to participate. I join in the traditional prayers of Sunday services, but I don't pray privately.

Toward the end of the intro course, we came to the Nicene Creed. I thought the moment of truth had arrived. Time for Rector Adams to explain how Episcopalians can profess the unbelievable every Sunday morning. Adams began by pointing out that the Nicene Creed had been the product of political compromise among contending factions in the early Church. Viewed from that perspective, the words of the Creed carry lesser authority than the Ten Commandments, which, according to the Bible, were given directly by God to Moses on tablets of stone.

Jim Adams went on to note that people in the fourth century had an easier time believing in miraculous happenings like the virgin birth and the Resurrection of Christ than they do today. The same could be said of people living in the nineteenth century—of anyone who lived before Darwin, Freud, and Einstein. We seemed to be headed into a historical interpretation of the Nicene Creed. I wondered if there would be anything left of it when we got through.

Jim wrote the phrases of the Creed on sheets of newsprint. Then he asked us to raise our hands when he came to a phrase we had a problem with. At the first phrase—"I believe in God"—my hand went up, alone. As we progressed, phrase by phrase, through the ancient text, more hands went up. Adams kept score on the newsprint. When we had finished the poll, "Born of the Virgin Mary" had won by a wide margin.

Jim suggested that the Creed need not be taken literally—that many, probably most, Episcopalians don't take it that way. The Creed has levels of meaning beyond the literal and historical. It can be understood as an expression of people's need for coherence and meaning in their lives. As Adams put it in his book about skeptics: "The Creed is not a series of propositions that the congregation claims to hold as a description of God. Any statement about God is bound to be both inaccurate and incomplete. In reciting the Creed, the congregation is stating what everyone can know for certain, a longing for God that the images and metaphors of the Creed put into manageable perspective."

I had a mixed reaction to this. I was relieved to learn that I wouldn't have to swear belief in the Nicene Creed as a price of admission to St. Mark's. I knew I couldn't do that. On the other hand, Adams's historical and symbolic interpretations of the Creed, coupled with the suggestion that I could believe parts of it and not others, or reject the whole thing, seemed too pat. I was left still wondering what the Episcopal Church stands for.

The intro class ended with a Sunday evening cocktail hour and an excellent supper. (Episcopalians are not known for mortification of the flesh.) The conversation was social, covering children, neighborhoods, politics. No one spoke of the Virgin Mary. While the class hadn't been a bonding experience—it wasn't that intense—I had acquired a first-name acquaintance with fifteen other newcomers. As the class skeptic, however, I still felt like an outsider. It would be several years before most of that feeling dissipated, and it never has gone away entirely.

I went to Sunday services over the next several months, but that was the extent of my involvement. I wanted to take a couple of steps back before going forward again. The big step forward at St. Mark's is the confirmation class, which, for most people, leads to confirmation in the Episcopal Church by the bishop of Washington and to formal membership in St. Mark's.

Confirmation, the most ambitious and demanding class offered at St. Mark's, consists of fourteen weekly meetings and two weekend retreats. The class is usually taught by a priest—the rector or associate rector—and by one or more lay teachers trained in St. Mark's version of Christian education (more on that in chapters 10 and 11). My wife and I signed up for the confirmation class that began in the fall of 1982.

Associate Rector Anne Amy was the lead teacher of the class. Anne had graduated from the Virginia Theological Seminary, had been ordained a priest, and had come directly to St. Mark's as its curate—the first woman priest in St. Mark's history. She was married and, by that time, the mother of a baby boy. Scilla Adams, a lay professional in Christian education, was the other principal teacher.

There were fourteen people in the class—nine women and five men—three married couples and eight singles, from a variety of religious backgrounds. Half the class represented typical Washington professions: four lawyers, two psychotherapists, and a labor union representative. Two were officers in the District of Columbia Police Department. One was a composer of classical music. Another worked for an environmental consulting firm. Several were federal government employees. There was a withdrawn, rather strange man I will call Harold. Ages ranged from the twenties to the sixties. (St. Mark's doesn't put children forward for confirmation, believing that candidates for confirmation should be ready to make a mature commitment.) Almost all were college educated. All were white. Not a cross section of American society, but an interesting and varied group of people brought together by a shared search for community and meaning in their lives.

The confirmation class is billed as a doorway to full participation at St. Mark's, a rite of passage. Left feeling frustrated by the doctrineless intro class, the ex-Catholic in me still wanted to know what I was supposed to believe if I decided to become an Episcopalian. Once again, however, theology would be kept in the background.

We were told that the class would be taught "functionally"—that we would have to deal directly with real-life issues, which would help us look at our own values. (Functional education is described more fully in chapters 10 and 11.) The functional approach, which relies heavily on role plays and skits, can seem artificial and manipulative. The class sometimes felt set up and reacted with confusion and anger.

My memory of my confirmation class sessions had dimmed after fourteen years. I refreshed it with a visit to Anne Amy, now rector of an Episcopal church in Alexandria, Virginia. I also talked to three former class members: Bill Jordan, a lawyer and program manager with the Environmental Protection Agency; Josie Jordan, Bill's wife, mother of two young children, and a recent seminary graduate; and Francis ("Sis") McKay, who has a Ph.D. in music composition from the Peabody Conservatory and teaches at Georgetown University.

The weekend retreats had a cumulative intensity, so my clearest recollections are of the two weekends the class spent at Du Pont House (once a summer home of the chemical tycoons) in Rehoboth, Delaware, about a three-hour drive from Washington. We arrived on Friday night of the first weekend in time for a dinner featuring crab imperial, complemented by

wines we had imported from Washington. (We always ate well.) There was
a two-hour session on Friday evening, for which one member, an attractive
young lawyer named Betsy, arrived late without a good excuse. Those of us
who had learned confrontation in psychotherapy groups gave Betsy a hard
time—what was her *real* reason for not arriving on time? Later that evening,
Betsy announced that she was dropping out of the class, citing job pressures; then she got up and left. It seemed a long way to drive just to drop
out.

On Saturday morning, the teachers put on a role play. The class was
divided into two groups. Ann Amy and Scilla Adams each played "Ann
Church," who was cast as the organizer of a group trip to the Holy Land.
The role play went like this: The group assembles, excited about the upcoming trip. Ann walks in and informs the group that she has bad news.
She has been to the doctor that day, and her diagnosis has been confirmed:
terminal cancer, with no more than six months to live. The cancer is inop-
erable. There is no other therapy, and no hope. Ann falls silent, and the
group is left to react to her.

Ann is portrayed as someone struck down by fate. God doesn't care
about her, apparently. Nothing any member of the group says to her—about
cures, about miraculous cases of survival, about "being with her"—helps.
She waves aside their well-intentioned but awkward attempts at comforting her and stands mute.

The idea behind the role play was for the class to experience meaninglessness—first in Ann and then, drawing on their own experiences, in
themselves. Their futile efforts to support Ann were intended to raise another issue: where are you left when the best you have is rejected—what
do you do then?

People reacted differently. I can remember Scilla Adams (my group's
"Ann Church") rejecting whatever we said and my feeling offended by her
attitude. I don't remember pondering meaninglessness in my life, although
there had been times of that. But I'm resistant to artificial exercises like
this. I usually remain the detached observer instead of "getting into the
issue." This gives me a (perhaps unfortunate) partial immunity to functional education. I get more out of functional exercises involving real situations, without an artificial element (such as the men's facial massage
described in chapter 10).

Bill Jordan remembered being surprised and confused by the role play.
It seemed a radical and unexpected reversal of what the class had done

before. Part of him wanted to respond appropriately to the situation, but another part felt set up.

Sis McKay felt "incredibly angry" about the role play, seeing it as "mass manipulation." She tried to cut off the exercise by suddenly announcing that both Anns had died. This made the other members angry with her. Things were getting a little crazy.

Only Josie Jordan reacted as the teachers had intended. She felt "really engaged." Just four years before, she had undergone extensive surgery, suffering a shattering loss—her ability to have children—in her twenties. That experience and a necessary interval to assimilate it enabled Josie to relate to the meaninglessness Ann Church was feeling, and to having people around who wanted to help but couldn't. She knew from experience that all she could do was be with Ann Church.

Sunday morning of the first weekend, we were invited to go off by ourselves for an hour to write about where we found ourselves and how we felt about the class. Later, in the Sunday morning service, we would have an opportunity to read what we wrote. I was feeling angry and manipulated, so I wrote a harsh critique of the teachers and the process. I read my critique, which was echoed by several others, during the service, but by then my anger had begun to fade. Seated in a circle, we passed the bread and wine around, saying the ritual words: "The body of Christ, given for you. The blood of Christ, the cup of salvation." We "passed the peace" by hugging one another and drove back to our lives in Washington.

Josie Jordan recalled an evening session shortly after the first weekend as a doorway that changed her life. In Lewis Carroll's *Alice in Wonderland*, at one point Alice is in such despair that she falls into a pool of her own tears. Drawing on the Alice story, teacher Anne Amy had talked about the pool of tears as a metaphor for those places in our lives where we fall into despair and become aware of our need for God. And where, if we stay and let it happen, God's presence can touch and heal us. Josie realized then that she, too, had stood in a pool of tears when she had gone through her surgery. With support from those around her, she had remained standing in the pool instead of withdrawing, and she had come through her ordeal with a sense of a new beginning and new possibilities. Since then, Josie has taught confirmation class at St. Mark's four times and graduated from Wesley Theological Seminary.

Graduates of confirmation class seem to remember best those exercises that had a transforming impact, on the one hand, and those that didn't work at all, on the other. "Lifeboat on a stormy sea"—our assignment on Saturday night of the second weekend—fell into the "didn't work" category. We were divided into two groups and seated in ovals, resembling (the teacher said) the shape of a lifeboat. We were told that the boats were taking water, that provisions were running low, and that one person from each boat would have to go over the side to save the others. We had to decide who should make the sacrifice, or be shoved over.

We began to tick off the obvious points—who was oldest or sickest. Unfortunately, no one had terminal cancer. Drawing lots seemed a promising option. Suddenly Harold, the quiet one, went over the side of my boat voluntarily. Moments later, two people in the other boat followed suit. It was unclear whether their departure had been motivated by self-sacrifice or a desire not to participate in the discussion. In any event, the survivors were spared making a tough decision.

Our class enjoyed planning and participating in the Sunday service on the second weekend, selecting the hymns and dividing the readings among ourselves. First, we had also been sent off to find something to bring to the service. I like rocks, so I headed for a sea wall on the nearby beach— big, gray rocks, thirty pounds and more. I lugged one back to Du Pont House, looking over my shoulder for the Corps of Engineers. Others appeared with a leaf, a pine needle, perhaps a seashell. Sis McKay wrote a short piece, which she played on the out-of-tune piano, with the class circled around her. That was a nice moment.

The confirmation class ended two weeks later. Looking back on it, the class didn't change my basic outlook on life—partly because of my resistance to functional teaching methods. For me, the lifeboat drill remained a group of people sitting on the floor in Delaware, not a life-and-death decision. But I did begin to appreciate St. Mark's emphasis on real human problems and lack of emphasis on traditional religious doctrine. I didn't know any more about what the Episcopal Church believes than when we started, but I made several friends—a good trade-off.

Bill Jordan didn't see lightning on the road to Damascus. For him, however, the confirmation class was an important first step toward looking at his life in religious terms—not in abstract doctrine but in fundamental human dilemmas. Josie Jordan did have an epiphany experience, which has guided her life ever since.

Sis McKay finished the class angry and was a marginal member for several years. She came back gradually and came to understand the functional education process better. Sis has taught Sunday school and classes that centered on Bach's "St. Matthew's Passion" and on Mahler's music in the Visconti film *Death in Venice*. She credits the confirmation class with giving her a more questioning attitude, saying: "Religion is about making sense out of life. The old ideas no longer work for me."

Middle-class professionals in Washington, D.C., are highly mobile. By the mid-1990s, several members of my confirmation class had moved away. A few left St. Mark's for other reasons. Sarah, the environmental specialist, left for another form of religious experience: Sunday morning skydiving. Harold, the quiet one, left shortly after the class ended, apparently believing that he had been poorly treated. Several months later the church office began being inundated with unordered mail: books, magazines, records, all manner of junk. It seemed to the rector's secretary that she was spending half her time returning the cascade of unwanted material. Harold's signature was later discovered on the order forms.

As its name implies, confirmation class usually leads to confirmation in the Episcopal Church—a serious intellectual and emotional commitment. I finally decided to go through with it, even though I remained skeptical. By that time, I was taking a cue from Jim Adams and beginning to deal with the traditional liturgy and prayers in symbolic terms.

I went with most of my confirmation class to the Cathedral of St. Peter and St. Paul (also known as Washington National Cathedral) in April 1983. Bishop John Walker—the only black Episcopal bishop in the United States (he has since died)—led us in the confirmation ritual from *The Book of Common Prayer*. "Do you reaffirm your renunciation of evil?" That was easy enough, and I joined my classmates with an "I do." Then we got to the hard part: "Do you renew your commitment to Jesus Christ?" The prescribed response was: "I do, and with God's grace I will follow him as my savior and Lord." Years later, I don't remember what I said. Then Bishop Walker laid his hands on my head and gently slapped me on the cheek. He had warm hands.

Chapter 5

People

If you can't say anything good about someone, sit right here by me.

—Alice Roosevelt Longworth,
quoted in her *New York Times* obituary

Washington, D.C., is a city of careerists—a city of ambition, hustle, and pressure to succeed. People are identified, more than is usual, by their work.

Washington has more lawyers per capita than any other city in the United States, and probably the world. Scores of them come to St. Mark's. Some, like my friend Bill Repsher, work for the federal government. Bill is an enforcement lawyer for the Environmental Protection Agency who tries to make recalcitrant companies comply with environmental standards. Operating on his own time from St. Mark's, he's an intrepid leader of climbing, canoeing, and white-water rafting expeditions. Bill and I were members of a men's support group that met monthly for several years. I supported him through his separation and divorce, and he supported me through mine.

Karen Byrne left a big firm to raise three kids and practice law a few blocks from her Capitol Hill home. In her general practice, she deals with estate planning, divorces, tax work. Karen has served as counsel to the Vestry, the governing body of the church. She sings in the nine o'clock choir and works with the children's choir. We've been friends since we took a Christian education class, "Me and My Job," and commiserated about clients who don't pay their bills. The Byrnes are a two-lawyer family. Karen's husband, Peter, is a professor at Georgetown University Law School.

Bill Doolittle has been a partner in an elite corporate law firm in Washington. He served as general counsel and assistant secretary of the Air Force during the Johnson administration. During the 1970s, Bill was senior warden of St. Mark's. These days, he's a member of the associate rector's advisory committee and occasionally fills in as an usher.

One Sunday during his sermon, Jim Adams asked what he thought was a rhetorical question: which profession is most heavily represented at St. Mark's? He flourished a yellow legal pad, saying it symbolized that line of work. Several people said "lawyer," and Adams nodded. I disagreed, saying that St Mark's has more psychotherapists—symbolized, of course, by the couch—than lawyers. Adams called for a show of hands: nine lawyers, eleven therapists.

I met Rich Chefetz on the banks of the Rappahannock River in Spotsylvania County, Virginia. I was on a St. Mark's canoe trip when my canoe capsized, my left foot became wedged between two rocks, and my ankle came out looking like a tennis ball. Rich was then a family doctor. He improvised an ankle support, which allowed me to finish the trip. Rich later did a residency in psychiatry and developed a private practice with a specialty in multiple personality disorder.

St. Mark's has a special attraction for people in the healing arts: doctors, nurses, and especially mental health professionals. I asked Rich and his wife, Kathryn, a psychoanalyst, to comment on that phenomenon. Rich pointed to the work of Alice Miller in *Prisoners of Childhood.* Miller contends that many therapists had emotionally and physically traumatic childhoods and that they experienced further trauma when they were unable to "fix" their parents. For Rich, St. Mark's is "a kind of safe house for people who are exquisitely sensitive to their early injuries." Instead of having an authoritarian model, a God of harsh judgments, God at St. Mark's is both mother and father, a God who recognizes ambiguity, who acknowledges that life presents some hard choices. It's a place where a person can say: "If God isn't always sure about things, maybe I'm not all that bad. I'm free to feel okay about myself." Kathryn Chefetz agreed, adding that therapists are unusually introspective. St. Mark's attracts them by encouraging that trait.

Others in the congregation represent a broad range of professions. Ann Craig teaches French; her lawyer husband, Roger, owns and manages rental properties. David Kemnitzer is an architect. Linda Barnes owns a real estate agency. Charlie Brodhead is a stockbroker. Carol Blakeslee-Collin is a producer for public television's *NewsHour with Jim Lehrer.* Bertha Martin is a dentist. Hayden Boyd is an economist. Robin Holliday is a nuclear engineer and an aerobics instructor. Neil Gregory is a lobbyist. Louise Walsh is an editor. Tom Gresinger is an obstetrician.

Despite the diversity of professions, St. Mark's members have a lot in common when it comes to money, education, and—to a lesser extent—politics. Episcopalians have a reputation for affluence. The St. Mark's congregation doesn't live up to that reputation, but most members appear to be comfortable. We have only a few millionaires—the stalwarts of fund-raising drives—but there are a lot of two-income families that enjoy combined six-figure incomes.

There are other signs of prosperity. About half the congregation lives on Capitol Hill, where houses typically sell for $250,000 or more. Some members have vacation homes, sailboats, or other expensive toys. Sunday morning parking spaces are occupied by late-model cars and vans (the associate rector drives a Mercedes, but it's old). Tacky attire is more likely to reflect an exercise in taste than a budget constraint. People do lose jobs from time to time—the Republican takeover of the House and Senate in 1994 cost several St. Mark's Democrats their jobs—but they don't stay unemployed for long.

People at St. Mark's are well educated. Virtually everyone has a college degree, many have done graduate work, and Ph.D. degrees are not uncommon. Many members are thoughtful and articulate, read a lot, and are comfortable with ideas. A friend of mine, a retired cop and an avid golfer, left St. Mark's after a couple of years, explaining that he wanted to play more golf on Sunday mornings. I suspected his real reason for leaving was discomfort with the intellectual atmosphere.

Political orientation is a relative thing. I live in Takoma Park, Maryland, a close-in suburb of the District of Columbia about twenty minutes north of St. Mark's. Takoma Park attracts artists, writers, environmentalists, and counterculture types with beards and ponytails. The town is a leftist enclave that has declared itself a "nuclear free zone," where power mowers are cause for shunning, and a popular bumper sticker declares, "Friends Don't Let Friends Vote Republican." St. Mark's is conservative compared to Takoma Park, but it's a liberal bastion compared to Potomac, Maryland, or Fairfax County, Virginia. Although people don't register at St. Mark's by political party, their support of abortion rights and other liberal positions indicates the political leanings of the majority.

Most people at St. Mark's don't appear to fit in any identifiable group within the congregation. There are, however, three groups that have interesting stories to tell. We'll look first at the Jews and the group that almost isn't there—the blacks. The gays and lesbians are the subject of chapter 13.

Rich Chefetz, the psychiatrist we met a few pages ago, was one of a handful of Jews at St. Mark's in the mid-1980s. During the early 1990s, however, St. Mark's experienced a sudden surge in its Jewish population. Most of the newcomers, like Rich, are Jews who married Episcopalians. A skeptic like me feels an affinity with the Jews at St. Mark's because they don't accept traditional Christian doctrine either, yet, like me, they participate in the life of the church.

Rich was born in New York City and grew up on Long Island. He attended Hebrew school and was bar mitzvahed in the Reform Jewish tradition. His aunt Sally, an important figure in his childhood, had a number tattooed on her forearm at Auschwitz—perhaps one source of Rich's basic seriousness. As a child, Rich didn't feel safe in his neighborhood. He recalled how a Catholic kid around the corner "would chase me and call me names. That wasn't a lot of fun. That stays with you." Such harassment wasn't peculiar to Long Island. Commentator and erstwhile Republican candidate for president Pat Buchanan, the son of a Catholic family, has described his boyhood neighborhood in suburban Washington as a *via dolorosa* for Jewish kids walking home from school.

Rich talked of his experience in a St. Mark's confirmation class, which, ironically, "cemented my sense of being a Jew." Jim Adams was the lead teacher; he made it a class in comparative religion, with extensive use of the Old Testament. The class was the beginning of Rich's later practice of melding elements of the Jewish and Christian faiths in his religious observances.

During the first weekend retreat, Rich had balked at sharing in the bread and wine. Adams had then spoken of the tradition in Jewish culture of offering bread and wine to visitors and asked if Rich knew the *b'rachas*, the Hebrew blessings. Rich said he didn't remember them, and Adams turned to Gayle Harris, an Episcopal priest and another class member, who began to recite the *b'rachas* in Hebrew. Rich recalled: "All Gayle had to do was say the first few words and the rest came back to me. I said the *b'rachas* in tears and shared the bread and wine. I've been doing that ever since when I go to communion." Rich also says the Lord's Prayer during the Sunday service, but not the Nicene Creed. "I pick what I want."

There are two requirements for formal membership at St. Mark's: baptism and an annual pledge. Rich describes himself as a "loyal, pledging nonmember" because he has chosen not to be baptized in the Christian faith. "I'm a Jew. I have a Jewish mother and Jewish father. And I would have gone to Israel if the Six-Day War had lasted much longer. Those are my people." At St. Mark's, he feels he is valued for being a Jew. "If you're Jewish, you're regarded as a resource for the community, someone who can see what's happening from a different perspective."

The Jewish-Christian Couples Group meets monthly for dessert and a program featuring topics of mutual interest. (Some Christian members prefer to call it the Christian-Jewish Couples Group.) A dozen of about twenty eligible couples—each made up of one Jew and one Christian—are active. The focus is usually on Jewish culture or religion because the members get their Christianity at St. Mark's.

St. Mark's is open to everyone in the community, but not everyone accepts the invitation. The population of the city of Washington is about 70 percent black. Once a fashionable white residential area, Capitol Hill became predominantly poor and black after World War II. Since the 1960s, streets close to the Capitol have been increasingly gentrified by white, middle-class professionals—the kind of people who go to St. Mark's. The Hill still has a large black population, but very few blacks go to St. Mark's. Since I became a member in 1982, there have rarely been more than five or six black members—about 1 percent of the congregation.

Verna Dozier, a black teacher, came to St. Mark's in 1955 at the urging of Rector Bill Baxter. Verna and Bill were colleagues as Christian education teachers. The District of Columbia public schools had been desegregated only the year before, and segregation still prevailed in District restaurants, stores, churches. Bill had assured Verna that St. Mark's—an all-white church since its founding—was ready for its first black member. Anticipating that she might not be greeted with enthusiasm by some of his white parishioners, Bill arranged for Verna to meet first, informally, with the Vestry.

Forty years later, Verna recalled that she had put on a dress for the occasion that buttoned all the way down the front. She had buttoned the top at home and had planned to button the bottom while a woman friend drove her to the meeting at the rectory. But Verna was so excited she forgot the bottom buttons. When she sat down in the rectory parlor, Verna noticed her omission and imagined what these middle-aged white men must be thinking: "Every black woman is a harlot." One of the most conservative members of the Vestry (who later became a friend) rescued the situation by saying: "This meeting is ridiculous. If Miss Dozier wants to join St. Mark's, there's nothing we can do to stop her."

Verna wasn't an activist, but she joined and she stayed. In the early years, she didn't expect people to embrace her, and most didn't. She didn't care if she was snubbed, and she often was. Contrary to Bill Baxter's assurance, it became clear to Verna that "St. Mark's wasn't ready for a black member at all." Gradually, however, Verna earned the respect and affection of the congregation. She served as senior warden from 1971 to 1973, the first woman and the first black person to be elected to that post at St. Mark's. Her tenure coincided with Rector Jim Adams's first sabbatical. During that period—according to the 1987 citation designating her warden emerita— "she guided the parish with an iron hand encased in a velvet glove." In a career spanning half a century as teacher, preacher, biblical scholar, and author of several books, Verna's influence has extended from St. Mark's to the national Episcopal Church and beyond to the Anglican communion, particularly as an authority on the role of the laity.

For all that, Verna Dozier walks humbly with her God. Verna is a regular invited preacher in the St. Mark's pulpit. She was scheduled to preach during my stint as a Lion (see chapter 6). Verna came to our sermon planning session, and it fell to me, Marianne Levalle, my co-Lion and a reporter for the *National Law Journal*, and our group to help her understand an epistle from St. Paul and a Gospel from John. As we carried coals to Newcastle, she listened patiently, took extensive notes, and gently offered a few thoughts of her own.

Bertha Martin, the second black member of St. Mark's, was born and raised in Selma, Alabama. I have some appreciation of her background, having spent time in Selma as a civil rights lawyer in the 1960s. Bertha moved to Baltimore as a teenager, graduated from Howard University dental school, and specialized in pediatric dentistry at the University of Michigan.

Bertha became a parishioner in 1969 when her daughter was taking lessons at the St. Mark's Dance Studio. She felt comfortable at the church from the beginning—despite being one of two blacks there—because she knew people whose kids were in her daughter's school or who were her dental patients. St. Mark's was hospitable to her skeptical bent: "If you had trouble believing, as I did, it was okay. I remember someone posting a cartoon captioned 'Where's God in this church?'"

Bertha's views on religion and race were nurtured during her childhood in Selma. Her grandfather, a Baptist minister, was "liberal about the Bible." He taught her how to play cards and followed the motto "If you want to drink, drink at home." Her grandmother was determined that she not treat people differently because of their race. Although the schools and churches were segregated, Selma was tolerant about race in some ways. There was very little residential segregation; blacks and whites mingled more and generally got along better. Bertha remembered: "I could walk into any store in Selma and try on anything. Everybody knew the family. When I came to Washington, there were certain stores we couldn't go into. When my goddaughter was baptized in the 1950s, I bought her a little dress at Garfinckel's. I told her mother I had bought the dress where I couldn't buy one for myself."

I asked Bertha why more blacks don't come to St. Mark's. She has lived in Washington, D.C., most of her life and finds that blacks "seem to cling to each other here." And they can be hard on those who don't. "I get condemned a lot because I go to St. Mark's. People say most of my friends are white." Bertha thinks that educated young blacks today—those who might otherwise come to a church like St. Mark's—aren't interested in integration. Black Episcopalians are going to black churches like St. Monica's on Capitol Hill or Calvary in Northeast. Bertha's opinion is confirmed by Eleanor Holmes Norton, the District of Columbia's delegate to the Congress, who told a congressional committee, "I am a member of a 100% black congregation."

I'd like to see St. Mark's more racially integrated, and I thought there might be things we could do to attract more black members. Bertha had no suggestions. She added that if she were to walk into St. Mark's today, she probably wouldn't stay. People aren't as friendly as they were when she first came, and some don't speak to her. I asked Bertha why she thought some people weren't friendly. "I may be wrong, but I sense it's racial." I suspect (and hope) Bertha is wrong about that. There are people at St. Mark's who don't have much to say to me either. On the other hand, my experience can't account for hers—she's a nicer person than I am.

St. Mark's has no celebrities. We had a shot at one when Episcopalian David Souter came to town to become an associate justice of the U.S. Supreme Court, located just three blocks from the church. On several Sunday mornings the justice was to be seen seated in the back, near the baptismal font. He always came late and left early, perhaps to avoid being recruited.

The last Souter sighting occurred on a fall Sunday when the nave of the church had been set up for Oktoberfest—a lively affair featuring pie throwing at the rector, overflowing mugs of beer, and oompah music. Later on, seeing an opportunity to attract real star power to the congregation, Rector Adams wrote the justice a note assuring him of a cordial welcome at St. Mark's. Souter wrote back, saying, "Although I have yet to settle on a parish that I can call home in Washington, when I finally do that it will probably be with a church rather more 'buttoned up' than St. Mark's."

Chapter 6

Liturgy—The Words and the Music

Wonder is the basis of worship.
> —Thomas Carlyle, *Sartor Resartus*

There is perhaps no greater hardship inflicted on mankind in civilized and free countries than the necessity of listening to sermons.
> —Anthony Trollope, *Barchester Towers*

I hadn't expected to be a Lion—at least not in this life—when a notice in the Sunday *Bulletin* caught my eye: "LION TRAIN-ING. Learn how to be a Lion ("Liturgy Is Our Nexus"). Lions lead our liturgy task forces which plan services, develop sermons, and select hymns. Seize this opportunity to grow liturgically. Four Wednesdays at 8." Having plenty of room for liturgical growth, I signed up.

Why lions, you might ask? Why not swallows or kangaroos? Because the winged lion, a mythical beast, is the symbol of St. Mark, the Gospel writer and patron of Venice, and, of course, my church. Faithful to that tradition, St. Mark's boasts an elaborately embroidered lion banner—a touch of the medieval—which is borne aloft in liturgical processions, behind the cross and torchbearers, and makes for good theater. (The lion symbol also appears in nonliturgical contexts. Members of the sailing club are Sailors of the Winged Lion. The Lavender Lions, St. Mark's gay and lesbian social group, is described in chapter 13.)

I had been attracted to the liturgy at St. Mark's from the beginning but knew little about it. I had only been reacting to what I heard. Jim Adams taught the Lion class, backed by several experienced Lions and the music director, Keith Reas. Adams introduced us to *The Book of Common Prayer*, the first Christian prayer book in the language of the common people and the official prayer book of the Anglican Church since 1549.

The Book of Common Prayer has been supplemented and revised from time to time and now runs to 1,001 pages. It prescribes readings for Sunday services, weddings, funerals, feast days—even for when a good Episcopalian gets up in the morning. It includes Old Testament psalms that are recommended as responsive readings in Sunday services. There are prayers for everybody and everything: for the oppressed and for the "good use of leisure," for cities and for "sound government," for agriculture and for rain. There's an ingenious index, a "Lectionary," which provides chapter-and-verse citations to Bible readings considered appropriate for each Sunday of the liturgical year—thus relieving the passive service planner of the need for thought. Like almost everything else in the Episcopal Church, however, use of the Lectionary is optional. There's plenty of room for imaginative and energetic service planners—the St. Mark's Lions and their prides—to put their individual stamps on the liturgy.

When I was growing up as a Catholic altar boy, there was only one Mass and it was in Latin. *The Book of Common Prayer* contains alternative "rites" for the Sunday service. Rite One is the more traditional. Its Confession of Sin conveys the flavor: "We acknowledge and bewail our manifold sins and wickedness which we from time to time most grievously have committed. . . . The remembrance of them is grievous unto us, the burden of them is intolerable." Rite One is appropriate for the gloomy season of Lent, or if you're seeking forgiveness for something really awful. But if you don't feel the need to grovel, you may prefer the simplicity of Rite Two: "Most merciful God, we confess that we have sinned against you in thought, word, and deed."

The Book of Common Prayer offers a choice of no fewer than eight Eucharistic Prayers for the celebration of communion. One prayer is cast in traditional and somewhat melodramatic language: "On the night he was handed over to suffering and death." Another is similar, but simpler: "On the night he died for us." A third ventures into modernity, focusing on the psychological drama of the Last Supper: "On the night he was betrayed." But each of the Eucharistic Prayers preserves the powerful language at the core of the sacrament, repeating the blessing that—tradition has it—Christ gave at the Last Supper: "Take, eat. This is my body which is given for you. Do this for the remembrance of me." And "Drink this, all of you. This is my blood of the new covenant which is shed for you and for many for the forgiveness of sins. Whenever you drink this, do this for the remembrance of me."

At St. Mark's, we call the most contemporary of the Eucharistic Prayers Star Wars because it speaks of "the vast expanse of interstellar space, galaxies, suns, the planets in their courses, and this fragile earth, our island home." Although right on course in the solar system, the authors of Star Wars were insensitive to gender issues. As the congregation approaches the altar for communion, the Star Wars liturgy calls on the "Lord God of our fathers, God of Abraham, Isaac, and Jacob," suggesting that communion is for men only. When Star Wars is chosen for the Sunday service, political correctness—St. Mark's style—is thought to require an amendment to its text, and biblical heroines "Deborah, Ruth, and Esther" are added for the sake of balance. It would be churlish to object to this amendment, but some things done at St. Mark's in the name of political correctness have sacrificed more important values. Take the case of John Donne and Buzz March.

John Donne (1573–1631) was, I think, the greatest poet of Renaissance England and the second-greatest, after Shakespeare, in all of English literature. Donne was a womanizer and carouser as a young man. An early poem commemorates the unintended pregnancy of his girlfriend and subsequent secret wedding:

> John Donne,
> Anne Donne,
> Undone.

But Donne later mended his ways and was ordained an Anglican priest. He eventually became dean of St. Paul's Cathedral in London, where he wrote a series of prose "Meditations." Donne's Meditation XVII reads, in part: "No man is an island, entire of itself; every man is a piece of the continent, a part of the main. . . . Any man's death diminishes me because I am involved in mankind; and therefore never send to know for whom the bell tolls; it tolls for thee."

This passage is among the most moving in the English language. As a member of a liturgy task force, I recommended that it be read preceding the Gospel, instead of the customary Bible reading. The task force went along with my recommendation, and Buzz March, a highly respected member of St. Mark's with the beard and bearing of an Old Testament prophet, agreed to do the reading.

Sunday morning came, Buzz mounted the pulpit and declared, "No *person* is an island." I was shocked and dismayed. The poetry of Donne's Meditation had been utterly destroyed. Worse than that, the great poet had been misrepresented; Donne would never have ruined his own line with "person." I buttonholed Buzz after the service and told him, in some heat, what I thought. Buzz remained calm, secure in his belief that Donne's sexist text had to be sanitized for St. Mark's consumption.

Sermon planning is a key part of the work of a liturgy task force. The idea of convening a small group of laypeople to help the preacher (usually the rector or associate rector, occasionally a visitor) find present-day meaning in ancient biblical texts is novel and—for the laypeople—a heady experience. Sermon planning at St. Mark's works like this. Having selected the Bible readings (usually with an assist from the Lectionary), the task force members study them to identify major themes that might be developed in a sermon. These are written down on newsprint. Enter the preacher, the person designated to deliver the sermon about two weeks later. A rather disorganized discussion ensues—a process called "brainstorming"—for about an hour. The preacher takes notes, which, in theory, will shape the sermon. It's understood, however, that the preacher is free to use the task force discussion to whatever extent it proves helpful.

Some task force planning sessions leave a clear imprint on the sermon—in its overall theme, in the issues raised, or in illustrative examples. Others don't. I remember being on a task force that met to plan a sermon with Carl Harris, an adjunct priest who goes on disaster relief missions for the State Department. In the Gospel for that Sunday, Jesus speaks of his church as a "house of many rooms." Seeing an opportunity to put in a plug for skeptics, I suggested an extended "house" metaphor that would include a "room" for skeptics. Bart Barnes, the task force Lion, was pushing a different idea. Carl ignored both of us. He wanted to talk about his abiding love for Mr. Cat, an animal who had wandered into his house from the cold. Carl's sermon dwelled on his love for Mr. Cat which, as I recall, he somehow managed to relate to loving one's neighbors and possibly God. As far as I could tell, however, his sermon bore no relationship whatever to our planning session.

I asked Jim Adams about the usefulness of sermon planning from his perspective as rector and as the most frequent sermon giver at St. Mark's. He replied:

> To me, the most important thing is to find out where people's concerns lie. I've preached on subjects that I wouldn't have touched if it

hadn't been for the sermon planning group. For example, what do you think the Church's response to AIDS ought to be? Their stories can be very helpful: What's it like to be young and single in Washington? What's it like to be a young father? I consistently use more of their input than my colleagues because I'm old and I've run out of material.

People with a questioning approach to religion often say they come to St. Mark's for the sermons. Others—the more traditional believers—sometimes say they come in spite of the sermons. I think a sermon should speak to the real, day-to-day concerns of people (dying of cancer, drugs in the schools), not just spin out theological abstractions. Sermons at St. Mark's draw upon themes from the Gospel reading for that Sunday, but the emphasis is on present-day reality, not the immanence of the Holy Ghost or the boundless love of Jesus. Although sermons are cast in concrete terms, the congregation is expected to think. Associate Rector Susan Gresinger observed that "both Jim and I try to stay away from sermons that spell it all out—here's the answer, the good news. Some people accuse us of never giving them anything. Others say, Don't ever wrap it up neatly and tie it with a bow. So we try to work between those viewpoints."

In fifteen years at St. Mark's, I've listened to more than six hundred sermons—some wonderful, many of them good, some not so good. One of my favorites by Jim Adams concerned how hard it is to be perfect, that maybe good should be good enough. Jim has a knack for picking vivid examples. He quoted from a letter by a ten-year-old English boy, away at school, to his father. The boy wanted to convey his continuing efforts to improve. The letter, in its entirety, read: "Dear Papa: I have been nearly good and hope I shall be quite."

Susan Gresinger came to St. Mark's as our curate—a probationary position—in 1986, immediately after graduating from Virginia Theological Seminary at age forty-two. She had been occupied with raising three boys, and St. Mark's was, as she put it, her first "real job." Susan's intelligence, wit, and warmth captured the congregation and she was promoted to associate rector well before the customary interval.

Some of Susan's best sermons have drawn heavily on experiences in her own life in which she found herself vulnerable. One Sunday she talked about her return from Asia after her first marriage to a foreign service officer had failed. Another sermon focused on her close relationship with her grandmother. A sermon about our attitudes toward children began: "This is a sermon about saying yes, a sermon about saying yes to becoming a parent and raising a child, about saying yes to all children, and, ultimately, a sermon about saying yes to God."

I remember being moved by Susan's sermon and, at the same time, excluded. I can't say yes to God. St. Mark's sermons speak mostly to everyday life, but at some point God comes into the picture—not that He will answer your prayers, but that your "relationship with God" will sustain and somehow guide you through the rough spots. Of course, I expect to hear God-talk at St. Mark's. It is a house of God, and most of the people there are believers. When we get to the God-talk, I usually translate it into something I understand or tune it out altogether. But I wish I didn't always have to translate or tune out. From time to time, it would be good to have the presence and views of skeptics (perhaps 10 percent of the congregation) recognized in sermons.

I voiced this complaint to Susan as we discussed the manuscript of this book over lunch. The following Sunday, Susan included the phrase "if there is a God" in her sermon. I was so surprised that I didn't hear what followed. During the comment period, I raised my hand and expressed my gratitude. She responded that she didn't just throw the phrase in to make me happy, but that she wanted to explore the implications of her sermon for skeptics.

Most people have favorite hymns, and others they detest. One of the good things about serving on a liturgy task force is that you get to pick the music for the Sunday service. Selections are made from the 720 hymns in the 1982 hymnal. There are usually four hymns in the Sunday service: one for the "processional" (the clergy and lay communion servers walk to the altar), one before the sermon, one during communion, and one for the "recessional" (the clergy exits).

My theory of hymns is simple: nothing good has been composed since the eighteenth century. "A Mighty Fortress Is Our God" by Martin Luther (1483–1546) is unquestionably the finest hymn ever written. No one has matched its melodic power or the hammer force of Luther's words—God against the devil:

A might fortress is our God, a bulwark never failing;
Our helper he amid the flood of mortal ills prevailing;
For still our ancient foe doth seek to work us woe;

His craft and power are great and armed with cruel hate
On earth is not his equal.

"O God Our Help in Ages Past" by Isaac Watts (1674–1748) holds second place on my all-time hit list. "Amazing Grace" by John Newton (1725–1807) is so popular it's become a cliché, but it's a wonderfully moving hymn. "Glorious Things of Thee Are Spoken" by Franz Joseph Haydn (1732–1809) is worthy of special mention. The hymns of Charles Wesley (1707–1788) are good, too.

Liturgy task forces serve for one liturgical season, usually about six weeks. Whenever I'm on a task force, I make it my business to get at least two of my favorite hymns on one of the Sunday programs. Before Jim Adams retired, I sometimes tried to slip in "The Battle Hymn of the Republic" because it's great fun to sing and because Jim hates it.

There are a number of unsingable or otherwise bad hymns in the hymnal. If the composer was a nineteenth-century Episcopalian with a name like William Croswell Doane or Vincent Stucky Stratton Coles, look out. I try, diplomatically, to block task force nominations of hymns that make my flesh crawl—particularly the inexplicably popular "I Sing a Song of the Saints of God." A sample verse:

You can meet them in school, or in lanes, or at sea,
In church, or in trains, or in shops, or at tea,
For the saints of God are just folk like me,
And I mean to be one too.

How's that for insipid?

Chapter 7

A Spectrum of Beliefs

Dogma has been the fundamental principle of my religion.
—Cardinal John Henry Newman, *Apologia pro Vita Sua*

In my religion there would be no exclusive doctrine; all would be love, poetry, and doubt.
—Cyril Connolly, *The Unquiet Grave*

I can't make the leap of faith necessary to believe in my own existence.
—Woody Allen, *Shadows and Fog*

*I*t's hard to find out what people at St. Mark's believe about the age-old questions: Is there a God? Can I experience God in my life? Is there life after death? The Sunday morning liturgy has become more ritual than profession of belief, obscuring what members really believe. People tend to talk about their religious beliefs in simple, personal terms rather than in traditional theological language.

St. Mark's has been known since the 1960s for a questioning approach to religious doctrine, an approach which has distinguished it from most other Episcopal churches in the Washington area. But most members would describe themselves as "believers" or "Christians." Thoroughgoing skeptics like me—agnostics who don't know if there is a god, but seriously doubt it, and who don't accept traditional Christian doctrines—are a small minority. During my early years at St. Mark's, we were a quiet, almost silent, minority. Tolerance toward skeptics was implied in the intro and confirmation classes, but St. Mark's didn't have an unequivocal policy at that time. We skeptics discovered that we could become members and participate in church activities, but we were surrounded by reminders—the wooden cross suspended over the altar, the saints and apostles frozen in stained glass—

that St. Mark's was a house of God, not a Quaker meeting or an ethical society.

Jim Adams's book, *So You Think You're Not Religious? A Thinking Person's Guide to the Church,* was published in 1989. The book has a simple thesis: everyone, including skeptics who may be *incapable* of a faith commitment, has spiritual and community needs, which a church is uniquely qualified to meet. Jim's book welcomes skeptics to the Episcopal Church. Following its publication, the intellectual climate at St. Mark's changed—open skepticism became acceptable, even though it continued to make some people nervous—and St. Mark's reputation as a church for skeptics grew.

St. Mark's has since reinforced that reputation by reaching out to skeptical people. Postings on the church doors invite "skeptics, agnostics, and atheists" to sign up for the confirmation class and to learn how to worship "without sacrificing your intellectual integrity." The tape on the telephone answering machine gives the times for Sunday services and welcomes both "skeptical people and conventional Christians." At a recent church dinner, a footnote in the menu "reserved the right to serve skeptics." Nothing like a little friendly joshing to make a skeptic feel at home.

By 1995, all the talk about skeptics coupled with the questioning approach that had long prevailed at St. Mark's began to provoke open opposition from the more traditional believers at St. Mark's. Vehement complaints were voiced in discussion groups at Shrine Mont—the site of the annual parish retreat in the Blue Ridge Mountains of Virginia. Some reported being made to feel uncomfortable, even stupid, by the skeptical people around them. Rector Adams had been surprised by the complaints: "I didn't know that there were any proper believers among us. I was quite taken aback to learn that was the case."

My first awareness of these tensions came when I signed up for a Christian education class titled "Thy Will Be Done." Most classes focus on problems of everyday living: caring for aging parents, adjusting to an empty nest, dealing with a death in the family. This class was unusual in its theological focus. I envisioned myself more as an observer than a participant— I couldn't honestly talk about the will of a God I didn't believe in.

At the first meeting, the class broke into small discussion groups. The people in my group seemed surprised when I told them I didn't believe in God. What was a skeptic doing in a God class? Later, when the class reassembled, several members expressed satisfaction at finally being offered a forum where they felt free to talk about God. They also expressed resentment about the skepticism that they saw as the dominant ethos at St. Mark's.

Now it was my turn to be surprised. At first I thought they were talking about me. As I listened, it became clearer that the speakers were complaining about a questioning approach to religion *by believers,* including the rector. Heaven only knew what they would think of someone like me, someone who doesn't believe any of it. Nor was this an academic discussion—these people were really angry. For the first time at St. Mark's, I didn't feel there was a place for me. So I dropped the class. One of the teachers later called to say that my viewpoint needed to be represented, and to urge me to reconsider. Not wanting to be a lightning rod for the resentments surfacing in the class, I declined.

All of this left me wondering about the range and concentration of religious beliefs at St. Mark's. The spectrum appeared to be wide—from traditional beliefs to agnosticism. But I had no idea how much agreement there might be on specific issues. How many believers in God (however defined) also believe in free will, in an afterlife of some kind, in miracles? Beyond specific issues, I was uncertain about the prevailing mind-set— unquestioning faith or a questioning approach?—and didn't even know whether there *was* a prevailing mind-set. When I decided to write this book, I wanted to find out, as best I could, what members actually believe.

Why not ask them? I thought. I had lunch with Jim Adams, who liked my idea of a survey on religious beliefs, to be presented to the congregation through the *Gospel According to St. Mark's,* the parish monthly newsletter. I drafted a two-page questionnaire and a short explanatory article. Adams suggested that I submit my drafts to the Vestry, the eleven-member governing body of the church, not for approval of content, but to give them an opportunity to consider whether the *Gospel* should facilitate an individual member's survey. The Vestry approved publication of my questionnaire, which appeared with the following explanatory note:

Religious Beliefs at St. Mark's

I am writing a book, tentatively titled *Skeptic in the House of God,* to be published by Rutgers University Press. The book will be, in part, a memoir of my experience as a skeptical member of St. Mark's since 1982. It will also look at the beliefs and experiences of others at St. Mark's. It will be hard to write intelligently about "skepticism" at St. Mark's until I have a clearer idea of how prevalent different shadings of skepticism are in this congregation. Although doubt or disbelief in the existence of God is the most common earmark of a skeptic, it's my impression that skepticism often implies doubt or rejection of other traditional Christian doctrines—such as free will, an afterlife, Christ as the only path to salvation.

I have prepared the following "VOLUNTARY SURVEY OF RELIGIOUS BELIEFS." I would appreciate it if you would take a few minutes to fill out and return this questionnaire. Your name will not be used in the book without permission. Some may feel that their personal beliefs are private information. If you're concerned about confidentiality, you may fill out your questionnaire anonymously. Thanks for your cooperation.

—Jim Kelley.

One hundred ten people filled out and returned my questionnaire, but some people didn't answer all questions. Highlights of the results are summarized next.

Belief in God

Thirty-six respondents—one-third of the total—believe in a "Higher Power." Close behind in second place were twenty-nine respondents who believe in a "personal God who listens to prayers and intervenes from time to time in people's lives." Twenty-one said that "God is within me." Thirteen (including me) described themselves as agnostics who "don't know if there's a god." One person described himself as a "Fundamentalist" and said that he had decided to leave St. Mark's, citing incompatibility. No one claimed to be an atheist, but, in typical St. Mark's fashion, eight respondents checked "none of the above."

Some highly individualized concepts of God came from members who provided their own definitions. Some examples:

- God is a metaphor for everything we don't understand, wish for, think of as perfection, dream of as possible.
- I believe in the reality of something I prefer to call the spirit. It is a power in all of us . . . as the eternal part of our being.
- I lean toward a Buddhist's goal of awakening or enlightenment— which I think I equate to "God," maybe?

- My understanding is constrained by language, time and place. "God" need not be so constrained.
- She may operate in planes which I cannot even perceive, and on a scale in a universe beyond my comprehension.
- I believe the word "God" has a useful meaning.

Belief in an Afterlife

Less than 10 percent of respondents believe in traditional concepts of Heaven and Hell. About 15 percent believe in a kinder, gentler afterlife: everyone goes to be with God in Heaven; no one goes to Hell. About one-third expressed belief in some other kind of afterlife. Some examples:

- When we die, we go hang out with our friends in the spirit world. When we've had enough of Earth, we go to other realms.
- This life is a learning experience—one of several stages or cycles in the wheel of existence. The ultimate purpose is to gain enlightenment.
- My immortality is what I have written, produced, created.
- A state where we can continue to grow without the things which fuck up the present life to a significant extent.
- You live on physically by recycling (we are stardust) and in the memories of those whose lives you touch.
- Nobody knows what happens after death, but the metaphor of Heaven is a powerful and poetic way of treating the painful subject of death.

About 25 percent of all respondents (including me) believe there is no afterlife—when you're dead you're dead. A closely related 10 percent say they don't know if there's an afterlife. Seven percent believe in reincarnation; their spirits will return in the bodies of other people or of animals.

Other Survey Questions

The questionnaire asked whether the respondent believes in miracles—such as the parting of the Red Sea and the Resurrection of Christ—and whether belief in Jesus Christ is the only path to salvation. Belief in miracles proved to be a comparatively close question: fifty-nine respondents affirmed belief, while forty-five said no. In contrast, a lopsided majority—ninety-seven to six—rejected the idea that one must embrace Christ to be saved. Many of these also rejected the concept of salvation.

Respondents were asked whether they believe in free will. Over 90 percent believe either in total free will or in partial free will, limited by environmental factors. Five percent (including me) believe free will is an illusion and that everything that happens is determined by natural laws. The illusion of freedom—what goes on in our heads—is, I think, brain chemistry. Finally, respondents were asked whether St. Mark's "tilts" too much toward skeptical viewpoints—in liturgy, sermons, Christian education, or in other ways. Seventy-seven respondents said no; twenty-six said yes.

Most survey respondents listed their faiths of origin, resulting in this breakdown:

Baptist	6	Jewish	1
Christian Science	1	Lutheran	3
Church of Christ	2	Methodist	10
Church of the Nazarene	1	Presbyterian	12
Congregational	9	Roman Catholic	17
Disciples of Christ	1	Unitarian	2
Episcopal	25	None	3
Ethical Culture	1		

As these numbers show, St. Mark's is a melting pot of religious backgrounds. Only about 25 percent of respondents are lifetime Episcopalians. About 60 percent come from "mainline" Protestant churches—Congregational, Episcopal, Methodist, and Presbyterian. Roman Catholics are the single largest non-Protestant denomination represented. The rest come from denominations ranging from fundamentalist-conservative (Baptist, Disciples of Christ) to liberal-skeptical (Unitarian, Ethical Culture).

Some conclusions about the survey: While concepts of God at St. Mark's are diverse, it's significant that some 90 percent of the survey respondents reported belief in *some* kind of God. Only about 10 percent described themselves as agnostics; there were no atheists. These numbers suggest that St. Mark's might more appropriately be called a "church for questioning believers" than a "church for skeptics."

The most striking thing about the responses to the "belief in God" question is the diversity they reflect, indicating that there is no core of religious doctrine common to the St. Mark's congregation. Only about 25 percent of respondents believe in a "personal God who listens to prayers"—the survey description closest to the traditional Christian concept of God. The slightly larger group of people who expressed belief in a "Higher Power," without any further definition, left themselves more room for their own ideas about a deity. And many of those who believe in a personal God or a Higher Power also expressed belief that "God is within me"—an open-ended concept seemingly remote from that of the traditional Christian God—someone "out there" in overall charge of things.

Almost everyone at St. Mark's believes in free will, leaving the door open to the traditional concept of sin as a voluntary act and to salvation as something one can earn by good behavior. As we have seen, however, people at St. Mark's have widely varying views about an afterlife—whether there is one, and what it's like.

Scholars of contemporary religion have identified growing numbers of people who develop their own religious belief systems, often within, or borrowing from, an established doctrine. While Christianity is the foundation of St. Mark's, two survey respondents, for example, expressed belief in some Buddhist thought. Scholars call this phenomenon "privatized religion" because people create their own belief systems which they often keep to themselves. For example, a person might choose to believe in an undefined Higher Power but reject miracles and any afterlife concept, or develop a private vision of an afterlife.

It's apparent from the survey that religion is widely privatized among the St. Mark's congregation. Privatization may even be the dominant mode of religious belief, making St. Mark's a hospitable place for skeptics like me.

I was disappointed and a little paranoid about the response rate to my survey—about 20 percent of adult members. Even assuming that some members threw the *Gospel* away unread or lost my questionnaire behind the radiator, that response rate seemed to suggest that many in the congregation didn't like my book project, didn't like me, or both. I learned later, however, that a 20 percent rate is considered quite respectable in the survey business, and that the usual reasons for failure to respond are negligence or an aversion to all surveys. And unlike a survey pitting corn flakes against oatmeal, surveys like mine always reach some people who have never paused to consider what they think and, as a result, don't know how to respond. After reviewing the returns and based on my fifteen years' experience with the congregation, I'm satisfied that they reflect a roughly representative cross section of members' beliefs. Jim Adams and the other members of my advisory committee for this book—all longtime members of St. Mark's—agreed with that assessment.

In any event, I wasn't trying to conduct a scientific survey, with random sampling techniques and quantified margins of error. The percentages I've derived from the numerical results may well have large, unknown margins of error. For my purposes, however, it doesn't matter whether more members believe in a Higher Power than a personal God, or whether belief in miracles is a majority or minority view. Even assuming large errors, the survey results demonstrate substantial support for all of those beliefs. More important, they demonstrate extraordinary diversity of belief at St. Mark's.

I tried to flesh out the survey results with interviews of several thoughtful people at St. Mark's, starting at the top. Rector Jim Adams said that he usually calls himself an agnostic. He has had "experiences of a profound nature," and he "uses the word God to think about them." He cited as an example "moments when I was falling apart and something was holding me together." He doesn't have any way to describe such experiences "other than in religious language," but he doesn't think there was "somebody out there who was intervening in my life."

Jim's "best guess" about the afterlife question is "lights out, oblivion. . . . [But] being an agnostic, I can't rule out the possibility of some other experience or of getting recycled." He doesn't believe in miracles. "The idea of a suspension of natural laws makes no sense to me whatsoever." He believes in free will, that he makes real choices, but "so do spiders and wolves."

I asked Jim if there is a common doctrinal core at St. Mark's or in the Episcopal Church. His answer was no.

> What you have instead is a common core of practice. You can form a church around ortho*praxy* as easily as you can form a church around ortho*doxy*. St. Mark's is a good example. Our practice is very conservative—in our services from *The Book of Common Prayer*, in our organization. We study the Bible and church history. We take it all very seriously. The Episcopal Church, going back for centuries, is more interested in orthopraxy than in orthodoxy. Anglicans have never been able to agree with each other on doctrine. And that's why I feel at home in the Anglican tradition.

Associate Rector Susan Gresinger's views on the belief questions were similar. Like Jim Adams, she doesn't "know if there's a God." Acknowledging a seeming paradox, she believes that she experiences God, for example, in the natural world. "I need to direct my awe and wonder at whatever it is that allowed this to be." Susan offered some examples: "When interpersonal relationships are really at their best—whether in an intimate sexual relationship or when people in a community really care for one another in ways that go beyond our natural instinct to look out for number one. Those things feel to me like an experience of a force of love that isn't easy to corral, but it's there."

Susan doesn't believe in miracles or an afterlife. As she sees it, one good effect of such a view is that "this is it, and whatever you're going to do, do it now, get going." She points out that the Catholic Church has long used the afterlife concept "to get people to put up with the most miserable conditions. It's a manipulative tool."

Not all Episcopal priests are agnostics, even at St. Mark's. Charles ("Chuck") Jaekle is a priest, psychotherapist, and author of a recent book, *Angels.* He studied at Union Theological Seminary under Paul Tillich and Reinhold Niebuhr. Following ordination, he served as chaplain of North Island Hospital, a detention facility in the East River for hard-core drug users from New York City. Until his recent retirement, Chuck was the director of the Pastoral Counseling and Consultation Center, an organization he founded to provide psychotherapy and counseling by trained professionals through Washington area churches.

Chuck Jaekle assists in Sunday services at St. Mark's from time to time as one of several "adjunct clergy." With Susan Gresinger, he teaches a course in modern theology that includes works of Paul Tillich and several other theologians. As a student, I found Chuck's interpretations of these often difficult writers articulate and penetrating.

Chuck questions the dichotomy, frequently referred to at St. Mark's, between skeptics and believers: "I think it's the wrong formulation. I don't know any human beings who aren't skeptical and believers at the same time. This includes fundamentalists and evangelicals, people who affirm a lot and try to live as Christians."

I can't do justice to Chuck Jaekle's beliefs in this space—his views on the relatively narrow subject of angels occupy his recent book—but I can indicate his basic stance. He thinks of God as "the spiritual center of the universe." And he believes there is "an unfolding plan for human beings which is expressed in the life, ministry, discipleship, and death of Jesus

Christ." Chuck is a believer, and a strong one. Does he get what he wants at St. Mark's? Often he doesn't; St. Mark's has become "difficult" for him:

> It's the one church in the greater Washington area that is positively hospitable toward people who are having bad trouble articulating what their faith is about. I don't hear very much affirmation about what people really believe. Not what they're skeptical about, but what they really—honest to God—believe about God alive in the world. I keep yearning to go to a semifundamentalist church where I can hear a sermon, not about what people can't believe in, but what it is they can! That's what I'm looking for, and there isn't a whole hell of a lot of it at St. Mark's.

Like the St. Mark's clergy, the parishioners I talked to expressed different kinds and degrees of faith commitment. Linda Ewald is fifty-three, the daughter of missionaries, married, the mother of two grown sons, and an accountant at a major Washington law firm. She and her husband, Bob, a graduate of Harvard Divinity School who works for the Library of Congress, have a passion for Wagner and will gladly spend beyond their means for tickets to *The Ring*. The Ewalds have been members of St. Mark's for twenty-one years; each has served as a codirector of Christian education. Linda is soft-spoken, with a self-effacing manner that can mask her keen intelligence.

Linda recalled being taught to pray from a young age amid "a lot of talk about God." Her belief in God has since been "whittled away," but: "It's a need I still have. I don't know exactly where it comes from. I'm perfectly willing to admit its my hang-up."

I asked Linda why she believes in a Higher Power but not in a personal God who intervenes in human affairs. She replied: "When I was young, I believed in a personal God. Later, when I looked around and saw the terrible things that were happening in the world, I wondered how a personal God who cares about everyone could allow such things to happen. It changed my views about God." Somewhat paradoxically, Linda added: "I think that God must really believe in free will, that He's not manipulating everything. He lets things happen. In fact, we're quite free. That's scary, but it shows that He respects us in allowing us to make the choices."

George Keeler, a sixty-one-year-old doctor from Texas, was senior warden of St. Mark's when I wrote this book. His religious beliefs have gone full circle—from youthful faith, through disillusionment, to adult belief in a "greater power." George's mother was a Presbyterian, his father "a golfer." So his mother took the kids to an Episcopal church, hoping his father might come, too. Young George was expected to believe in God, so he did.

George and his wife, Kay, also an active member of St. Mark's, have three living children. Their infant son Peter died of sudden infant death syndrome when he was two months old. George's world was "turned upside down." As he saw it: "I was a good person, this shouldn't happen to me. I didn't know where to turn." Friends invited the Keelers to join a "discussion group" at St. Mark's, which turned out to be a confirmation class. George became deeply involved in the class. He recalled that by its end: "I had killed off God as a required presence in my life. I came to believe that horrible things can happen, that I survive in chaos, and that God wasn't going to be much help. That was a very freeing feeling. I was in despair over the death of my son, but I wasn't in despair over the death of God. I could go on with my life and not worry about God."

Later, however, George turned to prayer in times of personal crisis and found that his prayers were sometimes answered. He cited one example. A believer in holistic medicine, George had been recruited to be the physician at a clinic in Washington that offered chiropractic and acupuncture as well as mainstream medical care. The offer was attractive, but he was concerned that he might be censured by his peers for breaking ranks.

George went on a retreat to reflect on his dilemma. A guided imagery process had seemed to confirm his holistic direction. He had envisioned a scene where one of the disciples asked Jesus, "Master, teach me how to heal." Later, while he was sitting under a tree reading the Bible, a little spider had lowered itself from a branch above and landed on a passage which seemed to say that he was on the right track. George views incidents like this as "visible signs of God's presence."

Karen Byrne, the lawyer you met first in chapter 5, earned B.A. and M.A. degrees in speech at Northwestern and worked for several years with a program to deinstitutionalize moderately retarded people into supervised living and working arrangements. Now she practices law in the District. To Karen, the concept of a personal God who intervenes to save us from harm allocates too much responsibility to a deity. As she sees it: "If there's water coming in the door, it seems foolish to pray. What you need to do is close the door."

Karen prefers the term "creator" to describe God. It suggests to her that God is responsible for the ongoing process of creation, such as a tree dying of natural causes. But her Higher Power is not responsible for babies being killed in Bosnia. People kill babies.

I asked Karen why she goes to church. She replied: "I go to take a break from all the trivia and demands I feel surrounded by at home and at work, for a pause, a contemplative moment. I go for the beauty which I associate with God. The architecture, the music, the language of the prayer book, the sermons—all are appealing and helpful to me. I have gone in times of crisis looking for comfort. I go to see people I like. I don't go to save my soul."

Tom Getman, fifty-five, is director of government relations for World Vision, the largest faith-based relief and development organization in the world. Tom lobbies governments to fund World Vision's projects in scores of countries, including Bosnia, Liberia, Burma, South Africa, and Palestine. As Tom describes it, World Vision sponsors development projects "in a transformational way, to create an atmosphere where reconciliation can take place." For example, in a project to rebuild Lebanese villages around Beirut, Druze and Muslim workers have been hired to rebuild Christian villages. Tom spends about one-third of his time abroad, primarily in Africa and the Middle East.

Tom is a rarity, a layman who lives out his faith commitment in his daily work. As a teenager growing up in Minnesota, he was drawn to people who "lived out the Gospel." He graduated from Wheaton College, a school in Illinois founded by Methodists which has retained its Christian orientation, and later from Fuller Seminary in California, an interdenominational school with an orthodox, evangelical orientation. Following seminary, Tom spent fourteen years as a staff professional with Young Life, an organization that works with unchurched teenagers—not by preaching but by example.

Tom knows the Bible. In the course of our conversation, he cited the Gospels of Luke and Matthew, Paul's Epistles to the Corinthians and the Galatians, and Revelation. His religious beliefs are traditional in many respects. Tom believes in a personal God who answers prayers, in the divinity of Jesus Christ, and in an afterlife. He also believes that Christ experienced an "actual bodily resurrection, that there was an empty tomb"; this is almost certainly a minority view at St. Mark's. But Tom's beliefs—the product of long study and reflection—go deeper than standard catechism responses. For example, his concept of Hell: "God does everything he can to let people choose between Heaven and Hell. But if he's a just God, he's not going to force them. Hell isn't a place of eternal punishment. It's a place where people can go who choose not to be in relationship with God."

These interviews underscore the diversity of beliefs at St. Mark's. In light of the survey responses, perhaps the only surprises are the degrees of skepticism expressed by the clergy, Jim Adams and Susan Gresinger. How can there be harmony in all that diversity? The short answer is: there can't— at least not complete harmony—nor would that be desirable.

At the beginning of this chapter, I described tensions that have surfaced recently between people from opposite ends of the spectrum of belief. The responses to the survey question whether St. Mark's "tilts" too much toward a questioning approach support two main conclusions: first, the overwhelming majority favor a questioning approach to religion; second, more traditional believers are a relatively silent but substantial minority— about 25 percent of the congregation. Some representative survey comments bring those contrasting positions into sharper relief.

For a questioning approach:

- I think the uncertainty and ambiguity that St. Mark's represents is an accurate reflection of the Christian religion as it's found in the New Testament.
- The combination of believers and skeptics is about right. I think we should talk about these issues and challenge each other more than we do. Mostly we avoid them whenever possible.
- I personally would not belong to St. Mark's if skepticism were not embraced. I mistrust believers.

For more traditional belief:

- I am a doubting Thomas, but now and then a firm stand needs to be taken to identify boundaries. All one's belief system cannot be amorphous.
- Sometimes sermons have more skepticism than religion—in which case I wonder why I spent my time listening. I can generate my own skepticism.
- St. Mark's is too dogmatic and rigid in its skepticism. I'd like to see more openness to the possibility of at least partial answers.

I think diversity of belief is healthy in a church, that debate about questions of faith and some resulting level of tension make for a vital congregation. Although I have remained a thoroughgoing skeptic, my mind is more open on religious questions than it used to be, and my respect for believers has grown.

Chapter 8

The Gospel According to St. Mark's

How beautiful upon the mountain are the feet of him that bringeth good tidings.
—Isaiah 52:7

Editor: a person employed by a newspaper whose business it is to separate the wheat from the chaff and to see that the chaff is printed.
—Elbert Hubbard, *Roycroft Dictionary and Book of Epigrams*

I realized during my first year at St. Mark's that if I wanted to be accepted as a member of the community I would have to do more than show up on Sunday morning. I like to write, so I joined the Editorial Board of the *Gospel According to St. Mark's*, the monthly newsletter.

Most church newsletters are as boring as birdseed—featuring inspirational pieces by the clergy, articles by parishioners about bake sales and fund-raisings, and thank-yous to half the congregation, by name, for various services rendered. Pages of the typical church newsletter are useful for starting a fire, but they aren't big enough to wrap garbage.

St. Mark's *Gospel*, while not a typical church newsletter, does include several standard features, starting with a monthly column, "From the Rector's Desk." During his long tenure as rector, Jim Adams, a gifted writer with an aversion to cant, commented on some aspect of parish life. Associate Rector Susan Gresinger, also a talented writer, produces a monthly column on some current parish concern or perhaps a reflection from her own life that touches the lives of others. There is a Vestry reporter who suffers in silence through monthly Vestry meetings to write an account of that body's proceedings. These standard features, over time, give a good indication of what's happening in the church; they occupy about one-third of the available space in a typical issue. The remaining space is given over to pieces by parishioners or members of the Editorial Board.

After a couple of years as a member of the board, I was named *Gospel* editor by acclamation, possibly because nobody else wanted the job. Donning my new editor hat, I wrote a piece calling for a diversity of voices, expressing my lack of interest in bake sales, and soliciting writing that "captures the spirit of St. Mark's." My philosophy of church journalism was simple: liveliness over godliness. Publish just about anything, as long as it isn't heretical or obscene. It didn't matter to me if a piece wasn't about St. Mark's specifically, or even about religion generally, provided I thought parishioners would read it—an approach which stretched the envelope of relevance. Several people complimented my vision (the only time that has happened to me), and a few submitted "spirit" pieces for publication.

During my term as editor, I increased my efforts—short of getting myself fired—to lighten up the *Gospel*. I was especially pleased with my yuppie version of the Twenty-third Psalm—written in response to an influx of yuppies in the mid-1980s—which began, "The Lord is my shepherd, I can have it all" and ended, "Surely I shall ski Aspen in April all the days of my life." My piece about the columbarium—the niches near the altar for the ashes of former members—combined black humor and practical information, such as vault size: "snug but adequate." I wrote light pieces about the escapades of the Bikers of the Winged Lion—the only motorcycle club in the Episcopal Church—which I had founded and rode with. Unfortunately, humor in a church newsletter is a perishable commodity; without sustained nurturing, it withers away. The *Gospel* of the 1990s has shown improvement in some ways, but it isn't funny anymore.

People at St. Mark's sometimes talk about carrying Christian beliefs outside church doors to their daily life and work. Rector Jim Adams suggested that the *Gospel* might make that Christian life ideal more concrete with a series of profiles of members trying to put it into practice. I took the lead by interviewing and writing a profile of Mary Lacey. An excerpt:

> Mary Lacey lives on Capitol Hill with a houseful of antiques, a harp, and a graduate thesis in an uncertain stage of progress. . . . Mary doesn't identify her faith with abstract religious doctrines, observing that much traditional doctrine "is hard for a rational person to believe in the twen-

tieth century." Mary's faith comes across as simple, practical and deeply personal. As she put it: "In a lot of situations in my life, I have been sustained by the thought that there is a spirit that moves and breathes and that if we look beyond ourselves in times of trouble we get some help. . . . I accept my friends who are Moslems, Jews, agnostics. I try to take people where they are and honor the best in them."

My Mary Lacey profile was accompanied by an invitation to members of the congregation to write profiles of other good Christians among us. Alas, no one accepted that invitation, so the Lacey profile was the first and last in the rector's proposed series. I came to realize that those who submit volunteer pieces for the *Gospel* are going to write what *they* want to write, not what an editor might suggest.

We published poems occasionally—some good, most of them bad. Peter Powers's haiku poem, which grew out of a church weekend, was among the best. Sample verses follow:

Two Days in October at Claggett

moonset and sunrise
together—the spheres conspire
to bless our meetings

valley of dry corn
weeds and mares' tails shoulder high
one barn, one graveyard

the meadow is full
of fat sheep, and fog and hope
rising with the sun.

We also provided a forum for younger poets:

What I Like About Myself

I like my home.
I like my train track.
I like my mommy and daddy.
I like Sunday School.
I like playing ball.
I like the way I look.

I like my fingers.
—Josha Jordan, age four

Always looking for ways to motivate more writers in the congregation, I proposed formal recognition of the best pieces published in the preceding year—Oscars without a statuette. "Gospel Board Taps Top Writers"
opened the envelopes:

Category	Author	Title
Best Piece	Tom Getman	Living in the Anterooms of Heaven
Best Commentary on Life at St. Mark's	Jim Steed	We Need a Parish-wide Distemper Inoculation
Sustained Superior Performance	Walter Dodd	Vestry Reporter
Best Written	Jim Adams	From the Rector's Desk
Best Poem	Susanne Bostic	Departmental Reorganization
Most Depressing Poem	Gene St. Germain	Jesus Suffering
Also Very Depressing	Jerry McKenzie	Cradle of Loneliness
Funniest Piece	Roger Craig	Hymn Abuse
Most Contrived Pieces	Vestry Candidates	Statements of Candidacy
Least Boring Class Description	Scilla Adams	Finding Your Way Back
Best on Outreach	Jane Byrne	Soup Kitchen Volunteer
Best on Sports	Jerrene Truett	Skiers of the Winged Lion
Best Historical Piece	Bert Cooper	More Than Rounded Arches
Least Relevant Piece	Jim Kelley	The Turtle and the Company Man

Lacking investigative reporters, the *Gospel* rarely contains fast-breaking news. Occasionally, however, an enterprising parishioner comes up with information we don't all know already. The Arkady Tyschuk story is a case in point.

In November 1982, Jim Adams wrote to the Patriarchate of Moscow for help in finding a church with whom St. Mark's could establish an ongoing correspondence "to promote peace and goodwill." In August 1983, Arkady Tyschuk, archpriest of Our Lady of Tikhvin Church in Moscow, responded, and the two churches agreed to a relationship.

The painting of Our Lady of Tikhvin, for whom the Russian church is named, is an ancient icon reputedly possessing miraculous powers to heal the sick and fend off disaster. According to legend, the icon was painted by Luke the Apostle, using Mary herself as a model. Thousands of the faithful come to the Tikhvin Church each year to kiss the icon and to pray for the Lady's intercession. The icon is said to have traveled widely in her ancient past—sometimes under her own power—from Antioch, to Jerusalem, to Constantinople, finally landing in the Russian village of Tikhvin. The Church of Our Lady of Tikhvin, located a few miles from Red Square, was built in the 1670s and topped with the typical onion-shaped spire, gilded to make sure God sees the church.

Every Sunday morning for seven years, the St. Mark's congregation prayed for the people of Our Lady of Tikhvin and for its archpriest, Arkady Tyschuk. We hung a reproduction of the original painting of the Lady next to the columbarium. *Gospel* articles by parishioners returning from visits to the Soviet Union described Archpriest Tyschuk, his family, and his church in fulsome prose. We sent a copy of each *Gospel* to Tyschuk to keep him current on our doings. We were under the impression that the good people of Our Lady of Tikhvin were praying for us, too. But all news from the archpriest ended in 1986.

In 1988, Collot Guerard went to Moscow on business but also with a charge from Jim Adams to contact Arkady Tsychuk. She found the Tikhvin Church one Sunday morning, but no Archpriest Tyschuk. Collot spoke at length with Kachuba Stephen Antonovitch, a sort of senior warden and administrative officer, who said he had never heard of St. Mark's. Kachuba reported that Tikhvin Church hadn't heard from Tyschuk for three years. He understood that Tyschuk was doing missionary work in Japan—founding Russian Orthodox churches in that Buddhist country. Grateful for that information, Collot gave Kachuba two St. Mark's T-shirts and left a letter for Tyschuk in the event of his reappearance.

St. Mark's never heard from Arkady Tyschuk again. Collot recounted her mission to Moscow in an eagerly read *Gospel* article, "Does Arkady Exist?" After that, the one-way relationship with Tikhvin Church was quietly dropped.

Gospel "editor" and "Editorial Board" were misnomers. Tradition dictates that just about anything submitted by a parishioner to the church newsletter is published—the chaff along with the wheat. Draft pieces are edited for grammar, typographical errors, and egregious redundancy, but not much else.

During my term and before, the Editorial Board's real job didn't involve journalism as much as logistics: getting the *Gospel* typed, mimeographed in seven hundred copies, collated, stapled, folded, addressed (including Arkady Tyschuk's copy), sorted by zip code, bundled, mail sacked, and carried to the post office—all with volunteer labor. Sometimes, most of the Board failed to show up for those chores, which posed serious problems. My pleas for help in the *Gospel* and from the Sunday pulpit went unanswered. Some of our readers might walk by the church office where two or three of us were collating, stapling, or sticking address labels on an issue. They might give us a friendly wave or an encouraging word, but they wouldn't stop to help. Nobody likes scut work.

The changeover to the present commercial system of getting out the *Gospel* is a paradigm of how many churches handle such problems—with volunteer labor as long as they can, with scarce budget funds only when they have to. By my second year as editor, I was fed up with cottage-industry methods. I proposed that we charge a subscription fee of five to eight dollars per year to cover commercial production costs, pointing out: "That amount compares favorably with annual subscription prices of other *au courant* monthlies—*SELF* ($28), *Playboy* ($24), and *Bon Appetit* ($15)."

The Vestry failed to act on my fee proposal. Instead, in December 1986 it voted $3,000 in budget funds to cover the costs of commercial production during 1987. After the January issue was produced commercially at a cost of $218, the Vestry—in a reconsideration of budget priorities—voted to take back $2,500 of the $3,000 it had voted for *Gospel* production only two months earlier. I responded with a "Here Today, Gone Tomorrow" piece urging action on our fee proposal or a "substantial infusion of volunteer help." Failing that, I threatened to "place the uncollated pages of the *Gospel* at the back of the church at the end of the month and people who want to make themselves a stale *Gospel* may do so." Enough volunteers showed up in the next couple of months—scare tactics often work in the short term—but not after that. One month, we carried out our threat. Few people assembled their own newsletters, and most of that issue ended up in the trash.

The tugging and hauling between the *Gospel* staff and the Vestry continued until the Vestry finally voted funds for commercial production. The present editors (now there are two) are free to focus their attention on their in-boxes—on the doings of the Vestry, on our companion congregations in Litchfield, England, and San Marcos, Honduras (see chapter 16), and on the bad poetry.

Chapter 9

Who's in Charge Here?

Politics are not the task of a Christian.
—Dietrich Bonhoeffer, *No Rusty Swords*

*M*any churches are dictatorships—benevolent to be sure, but dictatorships nevertheless. Authoritarian government is an ecumenical phenomenon found in Catholic and Protestant churches alike. Some Episcopal rectors are autocrats; the word "rector" comes from the Latin word for "ruler." But distributions of political power can vary widely among different denominations and from parish to parish—from dictatorship by the clergy to real political power in the lay congregation.

St. Mark's is committed to strong lay participation in church affairs, in collaboration with the clergy. Through an elaborate system of checks and balances, power over almost everything—from hiring a curate to choosing hymns for Sunday morning—is divided between the clergy and lay members. Major issues are rarely decided without a meeting of the congregation—the rough equivalent of a plebiscite. The democratic model is carried so far at St. Mark's that, according to Rector Jim Adams, his colleagues at other churches in the diocese are sometimes horrified at what goes on here. The system—if it can be called that—is untidy, but it works pretty well. And it appeals to people like me who are skeptical not only about theological matters but also of any centralized authority to whom obedience is expected.

Most of the power is vested, at least nominally, in the Vestry, an eleven-member body composed of a senior warden (the lay CEO), the junior warden (responsible for the building), and nine members—three of whom are elected each year for staggered three-year terms. There is no religious litmus test for Vestry membership or, for that matter, for any other lay office in the church. Any member in good standing who has pledged as little as one dollar can run for office. The Vestry approves the budget, hires and fires personnel, and sets general policy for the church. The rector presides over Vestry meetings but votes only in the rare event of a tie.

After five years at St. Mark's, including two years in a visible position as editor of the *Gospel*, I was favorably positioned to run for the Vestry, and I threw my hat in the ring. My motives were admittedly mixed. Vestry membership would move me beyond the fringes, possibly even to "player" status. I was attracted by the power and prestige of a position that didn't appear to require a lot of work. And (I should add) I believed I could do some good for the church.

Most Vestry elections are contested, with five or six candidates vying for three seats. That year, in addition to three full-term seats, there was a one-year seat to be filled to complete the unfinished term of a member who had resigned. In the beginning, my competition looked formidable. Matthew Black, a bright and popular Capitol Hill resident who had just directed a successful fund-raising drive, was weighing his candidacy. Worse than that, Lilly March, a resident saint and a stalwart of Christian education, was being urged by establishment types—a status conferred by twenty years' membership—to enter the race. Jan Lower, an able lawyer, along with lobbyist Janice Gregory and nurse Winnie Barnard, were all popular candidates. Steve Schindel, known for his annual charity walkathon to Harpers Ferry (the man can walk!), also declared his candidacy.

I ran a low-key campaign, with no organization. I wanted to win, but not enough to call everyone in the St. Mark's phone directory. I had at least a nodding acquaintance with about half the congregation, so I lobbied friends at coffee hours and mailed Museum of Modern Art cards (a touch of class) to others I thought might be leaning my way. As election night approached, Black and March decided not to run and Lower withdrew, leaving four candidates for three full-term Vestry seats and the one-year term created by the resignation. The only remaining question: who would get stuck with the one-year term? My confidence rose.

My election night speech featured several carefully polished one-liners and support for the sacred cows: Christian education and "growth" (undefined). I didn't have an agenda—sometimes called a "vision for St. Mark's"—reasoning that it might be dangerous to stand for something. Instead, I stressed my "open-mindedness" and "willingness to consider questions on their merits." Apparently sensing that the tide was running against him, Schindel announced that he would like to have the one-year term—thus removing what little suspense remained. The votes were counted, and Janice, Winnie, and I emerged full-term members of the Vestry.

Vestry meetings followed a pattern. We convened at 7:30 with an opening prayer, led by a member, and finished with a closing prayer at 10:00. When my turn came to lead us in prayer, I called for wise decision making, respect for one another, and the like, without directing my requests to God or anyone in particular. The opening prayer was followed by a half hour of "table talk," mostly about personal things—having a new job or a new baby, losing an old job, seeing a good movie. Our bonding done, there might be eight or ten items on the formal agenda, most of them accompanied by an explanatory memorandum. These items would be listed on a board with spaces for members to approve, disapprove, or call for discussion. Once an item received six initialed approvals—a majority—it was automatically approved without discussion. That part was a model of efficiency.

In a typical Vestry meeting, three or four controversial items might be discussed at length. Early in my term, discussion sometimes resembled a free-for-all because the floor belonged to whoever claimed it first and loudest. Once or twice I suggested that an aggressive talker shut up—a direct approach I had learned in group therapy. (It had worked better there.) Later in my term, the rector took more control of spirited discussions by recognizing speakers in turn.

Vestry members look upon the budget for the coming year as one of their major responsibilities. Most budget work, however, is done by the Finance Committee, a group of about ten people chaired by the treasurer and including several Vestry members who enjoy crunching numbers and shredding justifications for more money from the program committees. The Finance Committee addresses three basic questions: How much income will we have next year? How much do we need for basic expenses? How should we divide whatever remains among the program committee requests?

The income side of the budget comes from an annual fall canvass in which members are asked to pledge an amount for the coming year. The member's question, of course, is: how much? St. Mark's doesn't have any set amounts or formulas to answer that question. In 1983, a unanimous Vestry enacted 2.5 percent of income as the standard for pledging; for example, a family with $60,000 income would be expected to pledge $1,500. Apparently that Vestry was out of step with the congregation, which quickly made its displeasure known. Seven months later, the Vestry unanimously reversed itself, repealing the 2.5 percent standard and leaving parishioners to decide for themselves how much to give.

Over 90 percent of church income comes from pledges. Money from "passing the plate" scarcely covers the cost of Sunday morning coffee. When my wife and I became members in 1982, our first pledge was $400—about $35 per month. Our pledge increased about $100 each year until it reached $1,200. (At that point we separated and pledged individually.) During those years both my wife and I became increasingly involved in St. Mark's—in Christian education, in the Vestry, and in other activities. There is a strong linkage between involvement in the church and how much people pledge. Members of the Vestry will, generally speaking, pledge more money than any other group in the church. Marginal members, including some with substantial incomes, pledge modestly, while involved members are more willing to stretch. In other words, pledging is more a function of how much you care than of how much you earn. The average household pledge in 1996 was about $1,300—just over $100 per month—from some four hundred households (representing about seven hundred people) in the congregation.

There is also some evidence of a relationship between skepticism and modest pledging, even among skeptics who come to church more or less regularly. Perhaps they're as skeptical about how the church will spend their money as they are about God-talk. In any event, my experience suggests that involvement in a church will inflate a pledge more than skepticism will deflate it.

When I came to St. Mark's in 1982, the annual budget totaled about $150,000. The church has grown considerably since then, and most members have become more generous in pledging. During my term on the Vestry in the late 1980s, annual budgets ranged from $350 to $400,000; by the mid-1990s, they topped $500,000, giving the Finance Committee a largish pie to slice. However, the biggest pieces are spoken for.

Over half the money is needed to pay staff salaries, pensions, and benefits (health insurance has become a big-ticket item). The clergy and support personnel will get, at minimum, what they got last year, plus a modest increase to compensate for inflation. The only debate will be over raises—from modest to none. Other big pieces of the pie are eaten up by day-to-day administration, building operation and maintenance. There isn't much flexibility in amounts needed for heat, light, phones, paper, and stamps. "Cheating on the building" by postponing painting and minor repairs is a common short-term tactic that costs more in the long run.

After most of the pie is gone, the Finance Committee turns to the budget requests (wish lists) from the program committees—almost invariably for more than they got last year. The Worship Committee, for example, won't be satisfied with some new vestments; they'll also want fancy candles and hired trumpet players for Christmas and Easter. Community Concerns (the "outreach" people) had little support in the congregation during the 1980s and got only crumbs from the table. In recent years, participation in outreach activities—especially those with cachet, such as the Honduras trips described in chapter 16—has increased dramatically, and funding for outreach has increased as well. Most of the committees will get about what they got last year; some will get less. Christian education (chapters 10 and 11), the most important program at St. Mark's, doesn't have to come begging. That program is self-supporting; tuitions pay for weekends away, and Sunday school teachers buy the cookies and apple juice for their kids. As the Finance Committee gets down to the small change, it will spend a disproportionate amount of time on minor items—how to pay for Sunday morning coffee or an upgrade for the rector's computer. In due course, the committee will send a proposed budget to the Vestry for review and approval.

In theory, the Vestry reviews the Finance Committee's proposed budget in depth and puts its own stamp on spending plans for the coming year. As a practical matter, however, there's little the Vestry can do with the budget. Most of the money has already been committed to essentials. Even if it weren't, the Vestry members may lack the knowledge to take a hard look at a Finance Committee dollar amount. What do they know about the cost or need for paper, for which $5,000 might be proposed? And if the Finance Committee wants to give the clergy a 4 percent raise in addition to an increase for inflation, few Vestry members will have the courage to look the rector in the eye and vote against it.

In my three years on the Vestry, we made few significant contributions to the budget process, especially considering the many hours we spent talking about it. Two votes suggest the tenor of the Vestry's budgetary labors. In 1988, the nursery came to us for an additional $720. We were told that a second baby-sitter was urgently needed to cope with a baby boom on Sunday mornings. A spirited debate ensued. My extensive experience as a cooperative nursery school parent led me to wonder why St. Mark's parents couldn't take turns baby-sitting their own kids, particularly since we had just voted to cut funds for Sunday coffee. I cast the lone dissenting vote against the health and welfare of infants.

The following year, Nancy Donaldson, the doyenne of outreach on the Vestry, moved to amend the budget by giving an additional $1,500 to Community Concerns. It was pointed out that her proposal would unbalance the budget and "send the wrong message" to the congregation about the Vestry's fiscal prudence. Not to worry. Donaldson proposed a companion amendment to increase the following year's income by $1,500—the money to come from "an unspecified donation"—thus restoring the budget to balance. Her amendments were approved by a vote of 6–3.

One big financial decision did fall squarely into the Vestry's lap during my term: whether to undertake a major repair and renovation of the church building. The building had long needed new equipment and repairs. Grungy bathrooms couldn't accommodate the needs of a growing congregation. Ancient furnaces were rusting into the dirt floor under the nave. The furnaces were said to be dangerous—"sort of like sitting on top of a rocket." The air-conditioning system wasn't equal to the challenge of Washington in July and August. The wiring didn't comply with city safety codes; we could only have been spared an electrical fire by divine intervention. In addition, there was a pressing need for more space, especially for classrooms. Several Sunday school classes had to be parked on the parish hall floor.

Jim Meek, an engineer and then junior warden, formed a committee to assess repair and space needs. Meek also hired an architect to do a feasibility study, including cost estimates. According to the study, we could replace the heating and electrical systems for about $300,000. But since the basement space had to be opened up for furnace work, the study recommended that we go ahead and renovate the entire basement area for classroom, conference, and office space—at a cost of about $1 million. Allowances for contingencies, architect fees, and the unanticipated misfortunes that accompany such projects pushed estimated costs to about $1.5 million. Heady stuff for a Vestry accustomed to scrambling to cover the cost of coffee!

It was clear that we had to fix the furnace and the wiring, but I was skeptical about the rest. I thought the entire project would probably cost even more than $1.5 million. (Events would prove me right about that.) Where was a church that barely paid its bills going to get that kind of money? The Vestry repaired to Blue Ridge Summit—a charming old summer house with sagging staircases and lumpy beds near Camp David—for its annual weekend retreat to ponder the renovation. We decided at the outset that we would reach a definite decision, one way or the other.

Vestry member Louise Walsh later captured the spirit of the weekend in a *Gospel* article:

> The work sessions were hard, noisy, painful, frustrating and, in the end, joyous. We had all the options before us. Slowly we saw that there were no shortcuts, no way to postpone action. We could not simply throw it to the parish for a decision until we answered the hard questions ourselves. As the weekend neared its close, we were asked to write up our visions in small groups. Some of us were wary of pie-in-the-sky proposals. We were being asked to dream and that was hard. One of the groups offered us this vision of what we could be: "a vital outgoing community; the whole building as uplifting as the nave; a bathroom you'd want to read in; a sense that you've protected our heritage and left a legacy."

As the weekend wound down, I was surprised to find myself supporting the big-ticket project. My friend Woody Osborne, our senior warden, graciously included me in a description of the renovation project that was later placed in a time capsule for the St. Mark's bicentennial in 2088:

> Late Saturday night, Jim Kelley said he wanted to see whatever it was we were proposing to do put in writing. Jim was a natural skeptic, and an intelligent one at that. Even though I had gone into the weekend determined that we needed to go forward, I frequently found myself brought up short by his position that we were overreaching, and for an unnecessary cause at that. To my surprise, however, when the proposal was put down on newsprint before us, Jim responded in the most concrete way he could: he made a generous pledge right there on the spot.

"The Centennial Legacy Campaign" to raise $1.5 million (later $2 million) was an enormous success, due in large part to the services of professional fund-raisers who advised us to get most of what we needed up front from those few people in the congregation with real money. The fat cats were identified and solicited informally before the campaign was officially under way, enabling the campaign cochairs to announce at a kick-off dinner that we already had over $800,000 in pledges. One wealthy parishioner, a frugal single woman with extensive holdings on Capitol Hill, signed a challenge grant for $200,000. That left about $500,000 for the rest of us to come up with (until the cost overruns began). My wife and I pledged $5,000, about average for people in our circumstances.

By the time the Port-a-Johns left the parking lot and the drywall dust settled, costs exceeded $2 million and we had to take out a twenty-year mortgage for $800,000, leaving us with annual payments of $73,000. The project disrupted normal church activities for many months. Mud was tracked everywhere. We had promised the contractor we would never interrupt work. That promise was broken in the middle of a funeral when Mary Lou Kaufman—all five feet of her—marched down to the basement and ordered the men with jackhammers to cease and desist.

The improvements proved to be well worth the cost. Now the church is warm in winter, cool in summer, and the bathrooms are a pleasure to use. The dank and dusty basement is gone. In its place is an "undercroft" (a basement after a $2 million renovation) with classrooms, offices, a conference room, and a two-baby-sitter nursery. The renovated building helps us attract new members, who help us pay for the renovation and who, in due course, will help to support another renovation, which will help us attract other new members, who will . . . and so on—a Ponzi scheme for churches!

Vestry votes are an important but not a complete measure of who *really* runs the church. Rector Jim Adams is a shrewd judge of people and congregational politics. He possesses a charismatic and—when he chooses to show it—forceful personality. Asked to characterize his own leadership style, Adams said: "I try to be clear about where I stand, but I don't try to force my way on the Vestry or the wardens. I developed that style out of self-defense after I learned that you have to be brilliant to be a coercive, authoritarian clergyman and get away with it."

Former senior wardens who have worked closely with Adams are among the best judges of his political skills and leadership style. Ken Lee used an allusion to Tolkien: "St. Mark's is like the Hobbit. Jim was the squire who kept the shire safe. He *let* us run the parish." A suggestion from the rector can have a decisive impact. Lee suggests as an example that Adams might whisper in the ear of a potential candidate for senior warden: "What are you doing next year? I would have thought you might have heard the call for higher office." The potential candidate will probably take the hint, in part because, Lee believes, there is "a dependency relationship inherent in being member of a church. It would be nice if the top guy thinks I'm cool."

Although not a voting member of the Vestry, the rector frequently states his opinion on pending questions. As Woody Osborne, another former senior warden, put it, "There are Vestry members just waiting around to see what the rector thinks." Osborne recalled a time when he expressed an opinion at odds with the rector's. George Meng, another Vestry member, cast Woody a baleful glance, asking rhetorically, "You're not contradicting the rector, are you?" On another occasion, Osborne was sponsoring a resolution to require the Vestry to evaluate personnel, including the clergy, in executive session. Members he had sounded out before his proposal came to the floor had seemed to agree. During Vestry discussion, however, the rector objected emphatically to being talked about when he wasn't there. The vote was 10–1 against.

I learned the hard way about the power of the rector's office in the minds of others. St. Mark's pays its rector in accordance with diocesan guidelines, but the leadership doesn't like to tell the rank and file how much. There is a perception that clergy aren't supposed to make a good living and that pledging might suffer if the congregation thought the rector were being overpaid. The Finance Committee and compliant Vestries developed a practice of obfuscating clergy compensation in the St. Mark's annual budget—most notably by not including as income to the rector the rental value of the rectory (a lovely Capitol Hill residence with a rental value of about $20,000 per year) where he lives rent free.

I thought Jim Adams was an outstanding rector—worth all we were paying him, more if we could afford it. As a Vestry member, however, I thought, naively, that we should be candid with the congregation about all budget decisions, including clergy compensation. I proposed revisions of the budget format to include the value of the rectory as compensation and in other respects to make a clearer disclosure of what we were paying the rector. Adams supplied information but took no position on my proposal. Most of my fellow members of the Vestry, however, apparently saw my proposal as an attack on the rector and reacted as if I had contracted the plague. I worked out a satisfactory compromise proposal with senior warden Woody Osborne, which was adopted unanimously, if unenthusiastically—it's hard to vote against candor in budgeting. For two years after I left the Vestry, the disclosure requirement was complied with. Thereafter it was conveniently shelved—perhaps forgotten—and I grew weary of the battle. Nowadays, the congregation is told even less about clergy compensation than it was before. *Plus ça change, plus c'est la même chose.*

I don't mean to suggest that the rector always gets his way, despite the divisions of power in the organization chart. A few examples. During the 1980s, the big wooden front doors were in need of repair or replacement. Jim Adams wanted to replace them with expensive glass doors in order to project an open and inviting front to the world. Others opposed such modernity in a traditional church, as well as the expense. Following a heated debate, the Vestry voted against glass doors.

When the new organ was ready for installation, the best location for the several hundred pipes was much disputed. The choices were relocating the sacristy or taking over the library. The rector was prepared to sacrifice the library, but he failed to reckon with the forces of the contemplative prayer people who considered the library their sacred ground. The rector eventually caved on this issue and later confessed in a *Gospel* article titled "I Was Wrong."

Perhaps the clearest example of lay control occurred when Anne Amy, the associate rector, resigned to go to Germany with her husband and the position of curate opened up. Jim Adams knew whom he wanted for the job. Susan Heath is a bright, attractive, and likable young priest who had served as a seminarian at St. Mark's several years before. As a matter of canon law, Adams had the right to name a curate himself, without any participation by the Vestry or the congregation in the selection process.

Jim wrote an article in the *Gospel* listing his criteria for a curate and naming Susan as his choice. There were murmurings about the process, and a congregational meeting was called. Roger Craig, a former senior warden and sometime keeper of our democratic institutions, rose to argue that the search for a new curate had to be conducted by a lay search committee. Ken Lee, then senior warden, ruled Roger out of order, and Roger left the meeting. Susan Heath was then offered the job, but, to Adams's surprise and dismay, she turned it down.

Adams then told the Vestry that he intended to hire Thad Parker, also a former seminarian at St. Mark's, as the new curate. Adams's choice would have meant replacing the only woman cleric in St. Mark's history with a man. The Vestry took the position that another congregational meeting should be called. The meeting produced a consensus on two points: there must be a lay search committee, and the new curate must be a woman (so much for Thad Parker). A search committee was convened and eventually nominated Susan Gresinger as the new curate.

I remember the Sunday morning Susan Gresinger met with the Vestry for her job interview. I was there in the nave of the church to cover that newsworthy event for the *Gospel*. Susan was twenty minutes late, and the eleven Vestry members were starting to fidget. Finally she breezed in, mentioned something about traffic without sounding apologetic, and flashed a smile that captured the initiative. She fielded the Vestry's questions with ease, and, of course, she got the job.

Chapter 10

Christian Education Student

The journey, not the arrival, matters.

—Montaigne, *Essays*

I took the "men's class" in the fall of 1991 as my marriage was falling apart—a good time to hang out with other men. Toward the end of the class, the twenty-six members and four teachers went to Rehoboth, Delaware, for the customary weekend retreat. On Saturday morning, the class was sitting in a circle when the lead teacher told us to face the man next to us and to take turns giving each other a facial massage. I was paired with Bill Dickinson—like me, the father of two and no apparent threat to my masculinity.

I had never massaged another man's face before; neither had Bill. I went first, pressing my fingers and thumbs into the flesh of his forehead, cheeks, jaw and chin, down to his neck. and back to his ears. I was nervous and clumsy in the beginning, but after a while I began to get the hang of it. Touching another man's skin was a sensual feeling, but for me it wasn't the same as sexual arousal. When it was Bill's turn, I enjoyed the sensation of his fingers and hands moving on my skin, but it wasn't as if he were coming on to me. I chose to interpret my reactions as signs of sexual maturity. I can handle this, I thought. Looking back, I may have been suppressing sexual feelings I would have found threatening.

As an adolescent and young man, I had occasionally had disturbing thoughts about my sexuality. Looking younger than I was, I had been slow to date. I was a senior in high school before I kissed a girl. I've always been a lousy dancer—an enormous sexual handicap in the age of rock and roll. By the time I got through law school, I had almost, but not quite, lost my virginity. Most disturbing were the nightmares I had from time to time. I would sit bolt upright in bed, drenched in sweat, interrupting a dream of imminent physical contact with a man. My defenses always kicked in at that point, but I was left wondering about who I really was.

As I was turning forty, I became a member of a psychotherapy group—seven or eight men and women, all of us repressed to some degree. Two of the men—Jack, a lawyer, and Maurie, a Catholic priest—were gay. We spent a lot of time talking about sex, sometimes in graphic detail. When I felt safe enough, I described one of my nightmares. The group's reaction was a revelation. Relax, they said, you're perfectly normal. We're all a mixture of male and female. Most of us are predominantly heterosexual, but everybody has homosexual dreams. It's a healthy sign that you're not too repressed to remember yours. The therapist—who, I was sure, knew all things—agreed. I felt much better.

That was my background for the St. Mark's class. When we were through massaging each other, the teacher broke us up into small groups and told us to talk about what it had been like to touch another man's face. I led off by saying that, of course, a facial massage isn't like genital contact, but that it isn't a high five either; that none of us is all straight or all gay; and that massaging another man's skin has an intimate, almost sensual quality. I suggested we talk about whether the massages had felt good or terrific or disgusting, and why we had reacted as we had.

No one else in the group shared my perspective. One man said the massages were an exchange of favors between friends, as in: "My face is tired. How about rubbing it for me?" Another mentioned the comradery that can grow out of a joint activity—playing tennis or shoveling snow from a neighbor's driveway. The others merely nodded or said nothing. They weren't going to touch the sexual issues with a ten-foot pole.

I talked later with David Showers, a gay man (whom we'll meet again in chapter 13) and one of the teachers of the men's class. He recalled the resistance in the teaching team to the massage exercise. He had pushed for it because "that kind of contact begins to put you in a different place with someone." Based on his ten years at St. Mark's, Showers observed that "if there's any subject from which people will distance themselves real quickly, it's sexuality. They just don't know how to talk about it as a core thing that operates in all aspects of your life. If you're unwilling to talk about that—I don't care if you're gay, straight, bisexual, or whatever—it gets really warped and strange."

That afternoon the class divided into groups of four—two sets of partners—and the teacher explained the rules of an unusual card game. We weren't told to cheat in so many words, but the rules made it obvious that you couldn't possibly win unless you did. I wanted to win. We weren't allowed to confer with our partner, but I was pretty sure my partner, George Keeler, wanted to win, too.

The game got under way, and I cheated at every opportunity. So did George. It was quickly apparent that our opponents were playing it straight and wouldn't have a chance against us. We whipped their butts.

The postgame debriefing was revealing. One punctilious class member, a former seminarian, had thrown in his hand at the outset saying he couldn't bear the thought of cheating. George and I reported that winning had been satisfying and that cheating had been fun. As we saw it, we hadn't done anything wrong. After all, in this game you were *supposed* to cheat—a refreshing respite from workaday morality.

I was surprised to see critical glances in our direction from several members of the class—honest losers, I assumed. Roger Craig, a major player at St. Mark's who can be rather huffy, said that such unabashed cheating "raises questions in my mind about your character." That stung. Another winner in the game came at me from a different angle: "So you cheated. Why admit it and take all that flak?" Cheat, but don't tell.

The best Christian education exercises ("launches," as they are called) operate at more than one level. When my partner George and I talked about the card game afterward, I saw it as a way of looking at male competition: the drive to win is strong, and most of us relish the opportunity to throw away the rules. George, a doctor, agreed but suggested a deeper level. He recalled one of his patient's telling him that he was determined to get out of his job because he was being pressured to lie, cheat, and steal to get ahead. Similar tensions arise in all of our lives. We want to win, but we don't want to do it by climbing over the backs of our fellows.

That evening we were given an hour to write a letter to our father, telling him what kind of a father he had been to us. I felt that I had been through this many times before in therapy. My father had died just before Christmas in 1981, about a month before I started going to St. Mark's. He had been depressed, bad tempered, and lonely for as long as I had known him. As a kid, I was afraid I might grow up to be like him. (To some extent, I did.) My father became mentally impaired in his forties and spent the last third of his life mostly sleeping and watching television. My letter that night recited that stark history.

I went on to tell my father that he had never given me much, or so I felt. I recalled the time my wife and I had separated for several months when the kids were small. I had called home and asked him for money, and he had mailed me a check for $1,000. Later, during a visit to Iowa, he pressed me to sign a note formalizing my debt to him. I refused angrily, saying, "You never gave me a goddamn thing." My father walked out of the house, and my mother reproached me, saying, "You hurt your father's feelings." I replied, "That's what I intended to do." Knowing he'd never get my letter now, I told him I was sorry.

My letter recalled my attempts to reconcile with my father during the last years of his life—with some success. I was pleased to discover that, past seventy and living mostly in his memories—he liked to make lists of the members of his dental college class—he was still interested in sex. I had always avoided contact with his personal effects, but when he gave me a pair of used golf shoes he had mysteriously acquired (he didn't play golf) I wore them later for yard work. Toward the end, when my mother was having trouble taking care of my father, I flew to Iowa and took him for psychiatric testing in Minneapolis. The doctors said that he had extensive brain damage and should be institutionalized, but my mother insisted on keeping him at home.

I closed my letter by saying that he hadn't been a good father to me. But I knew it had been hard for him, and I was sorry he had had such a miserable life.

The class reassembled, and we took turns reading our letters aloud. A few reflected good relationships and genuine love and respect between father and son—what we all had wanted. Most were critical to some extent, and a few were harsh, though not as harsh as mine. Peter Byrne told me that my letter had "cut to the bone."

After the letter to our father, it was 10:00 p.m. The men's class had had a long day. We settled in front of the living-room fireplace with a beer or glass of wine. I felt isolated at first, having stuck my neck out farther than most about a lot of heavy stuff. But there were one or two others in the class who had heard what I said and wanted to talk.

The men's class in the fall of 1991 was the best Christian education class I've taken at St. Mark's. Several others were also worthwhile, and a few weren't. On the whole, however, the quality of the Christian education program is impressive. Some of the courses offered in recent years suggest the range and relevance of the program:

- "Forsaking All Others—the Costs and Promises of Marriage."
- "The Empty Nest—the Kids Are off to College."
- "Me and My Divorce—Looking for the Phoenix."
- "The Sting of Death—Dealing with the Death of Loved Ones."
- "Woman's Way—Finding Parts Lost Along the Way."

The basic approach to Christian education at St. Mark's is experiential—the operative term is "functional." The teachers don't have any right answers. The idea is to put people in real-life situations where they can work out their own answers, to help them, in the words of the St. Mark's mission statement, "engage boldly in the struggles of life." Issues are explored through role plays, skits, group discussions, and exercises like the facial massage in the men's class.

Veterans of Christian education describe the multifaceted program in different ways. As Rector Jim Adams sees it, "People are encouraged to become aware of how they function under pressure and of where they find the resources they need." Woody Osborne, a longtime teacher in the program, stresses the opportunity members of a class have to "look hard at, and accept the reality of, an important aspect of their lives." My friend Katharine Redmond, like me, is more interested in the people who sign up for a class than its subject: "I signed up for the forgiveness class this spring. Although forgiveness was not an issue for me at that time, I enjoy the opportunity to be with interesting adults and to talk completely frankly about my experiences. That kind of honest sharing is wonderful—so nourishing to me—and I find I can reflect my own experience off of it."

Classes at St. Mark's are accessible to skeptics and believers alike because they deal with difficult, sometimes gritty, issues from everyday life. Believers may learn how to cope with a wrenching experience—for example, a teenage child addicted to drugs—by finding their support in God. Skeptics, on the other hand, may find support to handle such an experience in the church community or in themselves.

There are, to be sure, religious elements. The classes raise fundamental religious questions, though not in traditional religious terms. As "Christian" education, the symbols and language of Christianity are sometimes present. For example, a class may conclude with a reflection based on a biblical passage. At the end of a weekend retreat, class members participate in a Holy Eucharist, the central symbol of the Christian religion. Skeptics can resonate to these religious elements in their own way. As John Lineberger put it: "Christian education is a kind of therapy if that's the way you choose to use it. If you're a skeptic, when they get into the God-speak you can glaze over and check out."

The program is not without its critics, including me. Peter Powers, the retired general counsel of the Smithsonian Institution and an occasional participant in Christian education, says that "for some, it's watered-down psychotherapy." Peter has a point. Christian education at St. Mark's does share some characteristics of therapy. People are encouraged to talk about their feelings (some don't need any encouragement) concerning emotionally charged issues. Since most of the teachers aren't trained as therapists, this might be a cause for concern. But the comparison doesn't extend to critical features of psychotherapy. Transference, the volatile emotional connection between patient and therapist, is much less intense and, for most, probably doesn't occur at all. The individual class member isn't subject to the kind of probing therapists engage in with their clients. Katharine Redmond calls St. Mark's classes "a kinder, gentler environment than a therapy group." Although strong emotional reactions are common—one indication that the class was effective—I've never witnessed a situation I thought was getting out of hand.

The Christian education program has enjoyed steady growth. The current program offers about fifteen adult classes and Sunday school classes for all ages—from toddlers to senior-high kids. Some three hundred adults, almost half the congregation, take at least one class each year. Ninety-eight people were involved as teachers or supervisors of teachers during the 1995–1996 Christian education year. The Christian education program's success, however, has made it something of a sacred cow. Sacred cows can do damage wandering about wherever they please.

Functional education principles are successful in small classes that meet over a period of time—usually weekly for two months. Such classes, the heart of the Christian education program, develop continuity and cohesion, which enable them to explore a theme in depth. It's quite another thing to attempt to apply functional principles to a large gathering (like the entire St. Mark's parish) or to a short-term working group (like a parish managers' weekend), which might otherwise get something accomplished. But that hasn't prevented Christian education's true believers from trying.

In 1985, the St. Mark's Vestry approved a proposal from the codirectors of Christian education that three major weekends—the parishwide Shrine Mont weekend, the Vestry weekend, and the parish managers' weekend—

"use functional education methods and understandings." (I was not yet serving on the Vestry, else there would have been at least one dissenting vote.) Let's look at what happens when functional education methods are applied to the annual "Shrine Mont Parish Planning Conference."

Shrine Mont is held annually in mid-June in a rustic Blue Ridge Mountain retreat. The conference is part social event and, prior to the advent of functional methods, part church business. One year everyone chose an interest group—fund-raising, education, or worship—in which concerns could be raised and proposals discussed and refined. That was a useful exercise. Then Shrine Mont went functional. Under the new dispensation, functional leaders choose a nebulous theme—such as "my community"—and concoct various exercises they hope will develop it. On a typical Friday night, for example, we might be told to break up into small groups to tell one another "why I came to St. Mark's." The next morning, the topic for discussion becomes "What keeps me at St. Mark's?" Further variations on these overlapping themes as the weekend progresses are supposed to bring us to a greater appreciation of our church community. In practice, however, we keep saying the same things all weekend.

St. Mark's has taught me the Christian virtues of patience and acceptance of unavoidable evils. I've attended Shrine Mont religiously for fifteen years. I no longer complain about the functional programs. Instead, I bring along a liter of California red and treat myself to a swim whenever the verbal fog begins to envelop the meeting room.

A Christian education class probably won't help a person who is profoundly depressed. One fall I signed up for "My Struggle to Be a Caring Person." It was a small class of perhaps ten people, two men and the rest women. "Caring Person" had no clear thrust; I can't remember anything we talked about, except the other man in the class. Bill was about thirty, neither handsome nor ugly, short nor tall, skinny nor fat—the kind of guy you wouldn't notice on the street.

The group went to an Episcopal conference center in Richmond, Virginia, for its weekend retreat. Bill and I were assigned to the same room, where we slept for two nights. He was quiet around me and reserved in the class sessions; when he spoke, it was in a subdued monotone. But I don't remember thinking that Bill seemed unusually depressed or that others remarked about his demeanor.

The next meeting night Bill participated in an evaluation of the weekend. The following week was the last class meeting. When I arrived, Penny

Whitman told me that Bill was dead. He had died of carbon monoxide poisoning. He had been found in the family room directly above the garage, where his car motor was running and the door was closed. According to the family, Bill's death had been an accident.

The class spent the last session talking about Bill and his death. Was it suicide or an accident? I thought the circumstances pointed to suicide, and I said so. Others in the class agreed. Penny added that Bill had been trying to date women at St. Mark's, including her, without success. One of the teachers reported that, in addition to our "Caring Person" class, Bill had been taking two other Christian education courses when he died. Only rarely does anyone take more than one course at a time. Although I had shared a room with him two weeks before, I didn't feel grief or see much evidence of it in the class. For us, the saddest part of Bill's suicide was that he hadn't touched any of us, or we him. Should we have struggled harder to care for Bill, or was he unreachable? I wasn't sure. I didn't go to Bill's funeral.

Chapter 11

Christian Education Teacher

Of all the animals, the boy is the most unmanageable.
— Plato, *Theaetetus*

The vanity of teaching often tempteth a man to forget he is a blockhead.
— George Savile, *Maxims*

In my second year at St. Mark's, the Lord decided to test me. He put Chuck Gregory, Sam Agle, and Benjamin Bruce in the third-grade Sunday school class. Then I received a phone call from Linda Meade, a codirector of Christian education. Would I be willing to step in and teach the spring semester of that class? Both teachers of the fall term were unable to continue (that should have told me something), and, being the father of a teenage boy and girl, I would be an ideal replacement. Linda went on to say that Lael Stegall, an experienced teacher, had agreed to teach with me, so my lack of training wouldn't be a problem. I had qualms and figured Linda must be desperate, but I couldn't say no to this first request for my services. Besides, I like kids—mine, anyway.

A few days later Lael, my experienced teaching partner, withdrew, citing pressures of work—another ominous sign. Only two weeks before the opening bell, I was asked to find another partner. Lania Bryant, a friend from my confirmation class and a sergeant in the District of Columbia Police Department, agreed to teach with me even though she had never taught anything but *Miranda* warnings.

The Christian education program includes a course on functional teaching methods, St. Mark's style, but neither Lania nor I had taken it. We were assigned a supervisor who gave us a crash course in lesson planning, class control (no corporal punishment, regardless of the provocation), and snacks (juice and cookies, no chocolate donuts). We were given a guideline on class content: about half the time for functional exercises and the rest for "lore."

Our classroom was next to the parish hall, furnished with uncomfortable chairs and a table around which our students were to discover their inner selves and their Christian heritage. Our class roster listed four girls and seven boys, ages eight or nine. Lania and I phoned the parents to tell them how pleased we were to have their child as a student. The class was scheduled to meet from 9:45 until 10:45 every Sunday morning—a whole hour to kill with Christian education.

That first Sunday we felt prepared. We had a challenging functional exercise ("launch" in functional education jargon): a role play in which a straight-A nerd in an honor-system school sees other students cheating and squeals to the teacher. How would the nerd feel? How would the cheaters react to the squealer? A scenario fairly bristling with tension and pregnant with possibilities for insight. On the lore side, we planned to tell the exciting Old Testament story of Jacob and Esau—about Jacob's clever disguise and his fraudulent purchase of Esau's birthright for a bowl of pottage (a precursor of lentil soup). We were holding the coat-of-many-colors story in reserve if our other material didn't fill up the hour. We had a gallon jug of Mott's apple juice (the good stuff) and two packages of Nabisco chocolate chip cookies. Let the class begin!

Sunday morning, 9:45, there were three kids in their seats—all girls. We handed out paper and crayons and asked them to draw an angel, a symbol of their behavior throughout the class. Chuck Gregory poked his head in the door, saw that his buddies hadn't arrived, and left to look for them. Several of our other charges wandered in and took seats. Ten minutes later, Chuck, Sam Agle, and Benjamin Bruce entered the classroom, all talking at once. Benjamin was carrying a "Power Ranger" equipped with a rocket launcher. There were shouts of "cool" and "neato" as Benjamin launched a rocket across the room. Thinking firmness was called for, I directed Benjamin to put his rockets away; he launched two more, then reluctantly complied. Then and thereafter, the boys talked simultaneously—about their real schools, their dogs, cats, lizards, and other creatures, what they got for Christmas, *Gilligan's Island* reruns—anything but the business at hand.

We had trouble casting the role play because nobody wanted to be the nerd. Jennie Kneedler finally agreed and played the role with aplomb. Role players "derole" afterward—describing how it felt to be their character—and the observers are then asked to comment on what the play brought up for them. Jennie, a gift to us from God, said that she had mixed feelings as the nerd. She felt bound to keep her promise to report cheaters, but she didn't want to get her classmates mad at her or make her nerdy reputation even worse.

Our role plays and skits played to mixed reviews as time went on—the teachers' fault, not the kids'. I blundered badly one morning when we were casting a skit depicting the story of Lot's wife, the woman who turned around for a last look at Sodom and got turned into a pillar of salt. We didn't have enough girls that morning, so I assigned Sam Agle, over his anguished protest, the part of Lot's wife. Later on, I worried that my insensitivity might have inflicted permanent psychic scars.

The lore part of the class—mostly Bible stories—went more smoothly because the kids were given juice and cookies while we read to them. The reading was followed by a discussion of the meaning of the story. To my amazement, that first Sunday reading about Jacob and Esau made an impression. Sam's mother, Betsy, told me later that Sam had brought the story back to their kitchen table. We went on to Daniel in the lion's den, Joshua toppling the walls of Jericho, Jonah in the whale, and other Bible classics.

The kids grew increasingly restless with the arrival of April and fresh grass on the Library of Congress lawn across the street. One Sunday morning, Chuck brought a soccer ball to class. One of the other boys asked Chuck where he had gotten the ball. Chuck cut him short with "None of your beeswax," suggesting that the ball had come from the junior-high supply closet. Not to worry, we thought, our class should encourage initiative, and besides, all the kids wanted to play.

Lania and I decided to try a morning of functional education on the playing field. There was a spirited game, and, for the first time, the class displayed real enthusiasm. Afterward the kids, with only a little prompting from the teachers, talked about their feelings of competition, the thrill of winning, and the disappointment of losing. Toward the end of the semester, there were fewer role plays and more soccer games. One morning the soccer game was rained out, so we took the kids to Sherrill's, a greasy spoon on nearby Pennsylvania Avenue, for chocolate donuts.

There were a few bright spots in my close encounter with the third grade. Overall, however, it wasn't very satisfying or much fun, owing to my lack of training (presumably fixable) and lack of patience (less fixable). Of course, the class was primarily for the benefit of the kids, not me. I don't know what they got out of it, and I was left wondering whether functional education methods should be used at all with young children. There are conflicting viewpoints on that question.

My former wife was active in Sunday school teaching. She had the advantages of training in functional methods, exceptional rapport with little kids, and patience I will never possess. After a year of teaching four- and five-year-olds, she wrote an article in the *Gospel* "assuring all doubters that functional education does work with little children": "I believe the functional education, the Bible lore, the playtime and snack time weave the fabric of our Sunday hour together. This has created an atmosphere in which the children have shared their deepest concerns with us."

Katharine Redmond, mother of two and holder of an M.A. from the Harvard Graduate School of Education, is also an experienced Christian education teacher. I asked her how functional methods had worked in her Sunday school class. "It's very hard for me to see how second or third grade kids can actually have a functional experience," she said. "But it's probably better than hearing about the lamb of God and memorizing biblical passages. When I grew up, you didn't talk about things that were embarrassing or painful. I think functional education gives kids a model to help them to be open about painful experiences." When I asked Katharine whether she would be willing to teach Sunday school again, she replied, "No way!"

The Christian education directors recognize that Sunday school teaching can be an ordeal. Most people interested in teaching want to teach adult classes, in which control isn't an issue, communication is easier, and the students are there by choice, not parental pressure. Perhaps most significant, the time commitment for Sunday school teachers is formidable: about three hours a week for eight months—counting class time, lesson planning, meetings with supervisors, and buying the cookies and juice. Teaching an adult class also involves three hours a week, but only for two months.

The directors minimize their problems in recruiting Sunday school teachers by making Sunday school a prerequisite to teaching adults; aspiring teachers of adults have to "pay their dues" first. One reason I had agreed to teach the third grade for a semester had been my impression that I would then be eligible to teach adult classes. At that time, the duration of Sunday-school teaching required for eligibility was unclear. When I inquired later about teaching an adult class, I was informed that the eligibility requirement had been "clarified": a whole year of Sunday school teaching. Disappointed but determined, I decided to meet the one-year requirement. But first I had to take the basic course for teachers in functional education.

Functional education as it's taught at St. Mark's rests on some rather elaborate theories about how people think and feel—theories I can sometimes find reflected in my own experience, and sometimes not. The detailed methods for implementing the broader principles are complex and rigid, discouraging those with only a casual interest in teaching. The beginner can get some help from the *St. Mark's Teacher's Manual*. Unfortunately, much of the *Manual* is written by the late Charles Penniman—an Episcopal priest and guru of functional education who never overcame his early training as an engineer, leaving him a stranger to the English language. Penniman tells us, for example, that he is "party to a multiplicity of decisions which [he] makes in the given ambiguities of the opposing tensions that life provides." Come again? Rector Jim Adams has attempted to explain some of Penniman's delphic pronouncements, but even Adams's keen mind and facile pen haven't made Penniman comprehensible—at least not to me. Despite their obscurity, Penniman's writings are held in near-reverence by many in the Christian education program at St. Mark's.

I don't pretend to be an expert in functional education, St. Mark's style—a concession with which the Christian education directors would, I am sure, heartily agree. My limited understanding can, however, convey a general idea of that elaborate process.

The process proceeds through several steps, from the conceptual level to interactions in the classroom. Teachers start by writing a two- to three-page "Problem Area Description" or "PAD," based on a "focus." According to the St. Mark's supervisor's manual, a typical focus for kids of elementary school age might be "Finding an even keel" or "Me in a limitless world." For an adult class about parenthood, the focus might be "What undergirds my success as a parent?" The PAD is supposed to reflect the individual teacher's experience "in the focus" and serve as a source of topics for classes.

Teachers are responsible for preparing a written lesson plan for each class. For that, they need an "issue"—for example, "I want the security of the familiar, but I want to explore new horizons." (I've made the irreverent suggestion that all functional education issues boil down to this one, which has done nothing to enhance my stature in the program.) Next, the teachers "dimension" (another noun becomes a verb) the issue by listing its "promises and costs"—a process designed to get the teachers' thoughts and feelings in sync with the issue. Some "promise" dimensions of the "security of the familiar" part of my example might be stability and peace of mind, while its "costs" might include lack of opportunity and boredom.

Ideally, dimensioning the issue helps the teacher to know what reactions to expect from the class and to guide the class to dimensions of the issue they might not otherwise experience. I suppose it sometimes does that. In my experience, however, dimensioning can quickly degenerate into a rote exercise, the objective of which is to write down three or four "promises" and "costs" on each side of the "issue" so that the lesson plan will be acceptable to the teacher's supervisor.

After dimensioning the issue, the teachers are to draft an "area of concern," which is supposed to summarize the dimensions in narrative form. I haven't gotten much out of this step either, but others more experienced than I have found it important. Katharine Redmond reported that the area of concern has often been a key for her. She described how she and her coteacher would tell one another stories from their own lives, which made the abstract issue come alive for them.

None of the steps we've looked at so far—focuses, PADs, issues, dimensions—are presented directly to the class. With those steps behind them, the teachers are ready for the most important planning step: the "launch." Launches—such as role plays, skits, direct participation exercises—are designed to get the students "into the issue" in a realistic, that is, functional way. The facial massage launch from the men's class (chapter 10), a direct participation exercise, is a good example. If the launch is effective, and if the students are not too heavily defended against it (as in the facial massage), they will recognize the issues it raises and see reflections of those issues in their own lives. Class discussion can suggest new ways to deal with those issues.

Under St. Mark's functional discipline, all classes are divided into five "units," corresponding to the dominant state of mind the students are expected to be in as the class progresses: curiosity (Unit 1), anxiety (Unit 2), hope (Unit 3), despair (Unit 4), and anticipation (Unit 5). Teachers select issues and launches appropriate to the unit. For example, on Saturday night of a functional weekend, the class is expected to sink into Unit 4—a time of despair, the darkest hour before the dawn. This is when a class about parenting might consider the birth of a Downs-syndrome child, or a jobs class might stage a launch about getting fired. In the world of functional education, Sunday morning always brings the dawn and, with it, anticipation of better things to come.

During the many Christian education classes I've taken since 1982, I've often failed to experience the state of mind the class was supposed to be in. If the Saturday night session involves a staged funeral, most of the class may arrive at Unit 4 (despair), with genuinely somber faces, maybe even tears. I'd probably look somber, too—out of respect for my classmates' feelings, not the deceased—but behind my somber visage I'd be wishing we could quit for the night and have a beer.

It's not fair, however, to judge the unit-mood concept by my frequently constrained reactions as a class progresses. When, as often happens, a launch strikes me as artificial or manipulative, my reality sensors kick in and I can't "get into the issue." Anthropologist Ernest Becker could have been describing me when he said of Freud: "He lacked the capacity for illusion. He saw things too 'realistically' without their aura of miracle and infinite possibility. The only illusion he allowed himself was that of his own science." I'd get more out of Christian education classes if I had a greater ability to suspend disbelief.

If evaluation of the elaborate lesson-planning regimen at St. Mark's were left to me, the results would be mixed. Talking to other teachers, however, leads me to believe that the system can work well in more experienced hands than mine. Ken Lee, a teacher since the 1970s, argues that the lesson-planning system, which I find so artificial and exasperating, is helpful to a lot of people in understanding the broader goals of Christian education. He points out that experienced teachers use the system selectively, stressing the steps most helpful to them. Woody Osborne, another longtime teacher and one of the most popular in the program, believes that the system "works well in getting the teachers [usually four in each class] on the same page," by putting them through a "common discipline." Woody also finds that classes respond emotionally more or less as predicted by the five units, citing a recent experience in teaching a confirmation class that belatedly arrived at Unit 3 (hope): "The first weekend was a catastrophe. They were all grousing at what jerks the teachers were. At the next class they were all happy. It didn't matter what we did, we were wonderful. They all loved each other. We couldn't figure out why. It just happens. That's the way life is."

When the teacher class was over, we were asked to sign up for the Sunday school classes we were willing to teach in the coming year. I signed up for junior- or senior-high classes—as far away from the third grade as I could get. Aside from my merits as a prospective teacher, I had been around longer than most of my classmates and I was pretty tight with two of the teachers, so I assumed I would be offered a job. To my surprise and chagrin, I was rejected—no explanation given. Failure to explain rejections to aspiring teachers remains a weakness in the Christian education program.

I thought I might have been found wanting because of self-deprecating remarks I had made in the teacher class about my turbulent ride through the third grade, or because I had been unduly critical of Charles Penniman, an attitude that some in the program would consider heretical. Or maybe the Christian education directors had reservations about my sometimes abrasive personality; would I bruise the children? In any event, I was out.

When teacher recruiting began the following year, I filled out a form (called a "druther sheet") expressing interest in teaching several classes, but the phone didn't ring. Ditto the following year. When I perused the roster of the chosen ones, I found a few to whom I didn't feel at all inferior. Pique and puzzlement were giving way to paranoia when my phone finally did ring. It was my friend Linda Ewald, a codirector of Christian education, with a request: the male member of the teaching team for the junior-high Sunday school class had dropped out two weeks before the fall semester was to begin. Would I step in once more? So this was my role in the program: Sunday school pinch hitter. I agreed, thinking I could relate to teenagers better than third graders and that the added credential should finally get me into the adult teaching program.

My skepticism hadn't been a concern in teaching third graders. Our approach to Jonah in the whale hadn't been calculated to raise theological issues. But I thought junior high might be different. During a teacher-training session, I told my discussion group what several of them knew already, that I was thoroughly skeptical, that I didn't believe in God or, for that matter, in any traditional Christian doctrine. I had no intention of volunteering my skepticism to the kids, but if we somehow got into theological questions I would tell them what I thought. I wondered what the reaction would be if parents found out that their kids were being taught by an agnostic (or, God forbid, an atheist) in Sunday school.

No one in my discussion group thought I had anything to worry about—partly because my skepticism wouldn't come up. (They turned out to be right about that.) Our class would be looking at real-life problems of youngsters entering puberty, not the Trinity or the Resurrection. Gardner van Scoyoc, a member of my group and an Episcopal priest, spoke to my concern more directly: St. Mark's represents a diversity of views, including skeptical views; our kids would be mature enough to understand that and to benefit from being exposed to skepticism. It hadn't occurred to me to think of my unbelief as an asset in Sunday school teaching.

Junior-high kids, age twelve to fourteen, are a breed apart from third graders. They're bigger, of course. They know more and think they know a lot more—boredom, real or feigned, is a universal characteristic. (When you're thirteen, you don't want your friends to think you're interested in something as uncool as Sunday school.) They gravitate toward cliques, especially the girls, and they can be cruel to outsiders. They're growing like weeds, exploding with pimples and hormones, and trying to hide their confusion.

There were twelve kids in our class when everyone showed up. They were bright and funny. Some were good athletes. The boys wore expensive athletic shoes (Nikes and Reeboks); the girls favored "Chucks" (cheap canvas sneakers). A few were handicapped. One boy had no arms, but he was a good soccer player and could write with his foot. About half were children of divorce who commuted between their parents' houses; some of them came only when they were staying with the parent who was a member of St. Mark's. In the beginning, most of the kids affected a laid-back attitude—as if daring us to come up with something interesting. They were difficult, but I liked them a lot.

I taught with Alice Cave, a technical writer later elected to the Vestry, and Margaret Wood, a paralegal with a big law firm. There wasn't a lot of teaching experience between us, so we tried to do everything by the numbers. In the beginning, we met several times with our supervisor. We got together on Wednesday night after work to plan next Sunday's class. We went through the lesson-planning routine religiously, if somewhat mechanically. We tried to get into the heads of our junior-high charges to find something that would wake them up and turn them on. Despite all that, the class started flat and mostly stayed flat through the Christmas break. We were getting discouraged and starting to count the months left to go.

Before classes resumed in mid-January, we junior-high teachers went with some fifty other teachers and supervisors, the Christian education codirectors, and the rector and associate rector to the annual teachers' weekend retreat in Rehoboth, Delaware. The purpose of the weekend was to provide a forum for the exchange of teaching ideas and experiences and to troubleshoot classes, like ours, that weren't working. Most of the other teachers reported success, exuded enthusiasm, and were eager to share ideas.

We came away from the weekend determined to pull up our socks and try harder. During the rest of the year we established closer relationships with the kids, and they became more involved in classes.

The junior-high kids turned out to be natural skeptics. One Sunday we went through the Nicene Creed, suggesting that they rewrite parts that didn't ring true to them. Like a lot of adults, they had problems with the Virgin Mary, but finally decided it was the Holy Spirit "who made Mary pregnant." Reflecting (perhaps unconsciously) modern psychological influences, they wrote that "God forgives us for the sins we forgive ourselves for."

"Banner Sunday" comes in May, at the end of the Sunday school year. Each class is asked to make a banner symbolizing its experience. I brought a pole from my garage, and Margaret contributed a bedsheet for banner material. Our kids balked at first—no ideas and no desire to engage in a childish exercise—until a mischievous kid with a morbid imagination I'll call Jerry suggested making a picture of the kids burning the teachers at the stake. Jerry's suggestion scored an immediate hit. The kids scrambled for magic markers, and we began to take shape on the bedsheet—death by fire at St. Mark's.

If Freud had been present, he would have observed that students who burn their teachers at the stake are expressing hostility. Yes, but it felt like friendly hostility. We joined in the fun as kibitzers, suggesting that the flames be made higher or that our expressions weren't sufficiently agonized. I winced when one of the kids wrote "nerd" on the male teacher (me) bound to the stake. I was touched when, a few minutes later, another kid marked the word out.

Last year, I was asked to teach the baptism class—a short course of four sessions for new parents. Most of the parents aren't regular members. They take the class to make their baby eligible for the sacrament, and many are never seen again. Janice Gregory and I taught the class, exhausting the topic of how it feels to be a new parent. After that, I had just about given up the idea of teaching a real adult class when Ellen Cardwell, one of the codirectors of Christian education for 1996, stopped me in the hall. Would I be willing to teach "The Sting of Death" next spring? "Sure," I said.

Chapter 12

Women at St. Mark's

Sir, a woman's preaching is like a dog's walking on his hinder legs. It is not done well, but you are surprised to see it done at all.
—Samuel Johnson, quoted by James Boswell,
Tour to the Hebrides, 1763

Whatever women do, they must do it twice as well as men to be thought as good. Fortunately, this is not difficult.
—Charlotte Whitton, mayor of Ottawa, Canada, 1963

I'm a recovering sexist. Like most men of my generation, I was raised in the traditional family structure: my father worked while my mother stayed home with the kids. Looking back, I wonder what my mother—an intelligent, educated, and energetic woman—did with her time after she cleaned the oven and finished ironing the sheets, underwear, and other things that didn't need to be ironed. Although I wasn't aware of it then, I must have developed something approaching disdain for my mother's menial contributions to the family's welfare.

There was another reason for my nascent misogyny. My father was a passive and disorganized person. Somebody had to take charge of the family. So my mother stepped up and took control of just about everything: money, dinner table conversation, even the tie my father should wear on Sunday. I was scornful of my father's passivity, but, even more, I felt threatened by my mother's controlling presence. No woman was going to tell me what to do.

Arguments with my mother—in reality, struggles for control—were outward manifestations of largely subconscious feelings that persisted into adulthood. The year after my father died, I took my wife and children to Iowa to visit my mother, then eighty. One day I told her I was on my way to visit the local judge, a former mentor of mine. I was wearing jeans and a sweatshirt. My mother insisted that I wear a suit and tie. I refused. She began to cry and retreated to her bedroom. I went to see the judge in my jeans and sweatshirt. Later on, I realized it wouldn't have hurt me to put on a suit and tie for my old and widowed mother.

Sexism was pervasive in the culture of my college years and my first jobs in the 1960s. At the University of Iowa the girls had to be in Currier Hall, the women's dorm, by 11:00 p.m. on weeknights. The boys didn't have to come in at all. Most of the girls were only in college for an "Mrs. degree"—or so we boys thought.

There were two women and over one hundred men in my law school class. After graduating in 1961, I took a job with a Wall Street firm in New York City. Only one of the firm's 125 lawyers was a woman. I never met or even saw her, but I was told that she did probate work—a genteel specialty thought appropriate for women in a man's profession.

After I got married in 1965, life fell into traditional patterns. I had a job; my wife stayed home with the kids until they were nine or ten. We had one joint checking account, which I balanced as soon as the checks came in. I always did our tax returns. I had no way to compare my understandings of spousal relationships until I spent several years in group psychotherapy with other married men and women. Although therapy mellowed the sexist in me somewhat, I sometimes thought the women talked too much. Amid the feminist rhetoric and bra burning of the time, I developed some politically correct opinions—the right to choose an abortion and to equal employment opportunities—but feminism wasn't something I got excited about.

After she became free of primary responsibility for our small children, my wife went back to graduate school. She got her career under way in her forties, after I had twenty years of lawyering behind me. About ten years after that, we separated and divorced, partly, I think, because of earlier and lingering inequalities in our relationship. In the meantime, we had joined the Episcopal Church—an institution which, like me, is a recovering sexist.

The clergy of the national Episcopal Church was an all-male preserve until 1976, when ordination of women was approved. Their numbers have increased sharply since then. Looking down the pipeline, we see that in 1996 about 40 percent of seminary students were women. The first consecration of a woman as a bishop occurred in 1989. By 1996, there were five female bishops compared to some three hundred male bishops. In sum, the national church is still dominated by men today, but it's opening increasingly to women and women's perspectives.

Attitudes toward women can vary greatly from one Episcopal church to another. A few years ago, I was in New York City for the weekend and happened to attend a Sunday service at St. Thomas, an imposing Gothic church on Fifth Avenue, around the corner from the Museum of Modern Art. The male rector and a supporting phalanx of male clergy conducted the service. The rector delivered a sermon deploring the upcoming elevation of a woman priest to bishop, a misfortune he viewed as subversive to church tradition. However, I've attended services at other Episcopal churches in New York City—St. John the Divine in Morningside Heights and Trinity Church on Wall Street—which appeared to be fully open to women.

Although not everyone would agree with me, I think that women and men are treated equally at St. Mark's—on the surface, if not always beneath it. Starting near the top (just below the rector), we've had a female curate or associate rector since ordination of women was first approved twenty years ago. Although St. Mark's has had male rectors throughout its history, I think the present congregation would be open, perhaps even predisposed, to hiring a woman to replace Jim Adams as rector after his retirement in 1996. (The selection process was under way as this book was completed.)

Leadership positions for key committees and programs, such as the Worship Committee and the Christian education program, are almost always filled with coleaders—one woman and one man. Efforts are made to include both sexes in committee memberships. Nearly all Christian education classes are team-taught by men and women. The same is true of the leaders of liturgy task forces.

Elections for Vestry and warden positions probably say more about gender attitudes because most of the congregation votes and Vestry seats are usually contested. I'm told that before I came to St. Mark's, men dominated those positions. During my fifteen years there, about equal numbers of men and women have been elected to the Vestry and to the highest lay office, senior warden.

There are only two exceptions to this history of power sharing between the sexes: the junior warden, who is responsible for building maintenance, is traditionally a man's job; and the Altar Guild, which folds altar cloths, decants sacramental wine, and performs other "female" chores, is traditionally composed of women. No respecters of tradition, women at St.

Mark's have challenged the first exception in recent years. Two women have served as junior warden, coping with occasional vandalism and water in the basement—another "man's job" lost in the battle of the sexes. Interestingly, two men have served on the Altar Guild during the same period.

Attitudes at St. Mark's toward abortion are another indication of the congregation's sympathies where women's rights and sensibilities are concerned. According to Associate Rector Susan Gresinger, a few members oppose abortion on religious grounds, but the congregation as a whole is overwhelmingly pro choice. Abortion issues have surfaced periodically in Susan's experience as a priest, beginning with her ordination.

Susan's husband, Tom, is an obstetrician who owns abortion clinics where he works part-time. When Susan was ordained at the Washington National Cathedral in 1985, Noel—the National Organization of Episcopalians for Life—a right-to-life group based at the Episcopal Church of the Apostles in Fairfax, Virginia, picketed the cathedral to protest her ordination. Before Susan was called to St. Mark's as its curate in 1986, she told us about Tom's abortion work and the cathedral picketing incident.

Twice during her first year, the Noel group appeared at St. Mark's to protest our employment of an abortionist's wife to minister to our spiritual needs. The Sunday morning of their first appearance, I remember being startled to see several men and women patrolling the sidewalk with placards saying "Dr. Gresinger Is a Murderer." Susan was preaching that morning. This is how she recalls what happened:

> I came to church with a sermon prepared. Someone told me those bozos were out there. At St. Mark's we insist that our worship reflect what's really going on in the community. For me to stand up and preach a sermon that had nothing to do with the building's being surrounded by people protesting my husband's work would have been a little out of touch.
>
> I don't remember now exactly what I said, but it was to this effect: Nobody is in *favor* of abortion. The argument is about who makes that hard choice—the woman or the government. The picketers' opinions should be respected. Their presence may be upsetting, but as long as they're on public property they're within their rights. And if they want to come in the church and worship with us, they're welcome to do that.

And this is how Susan felt about the picketers:

I felt attacked and violated. This is my altar. How dare they come here, especially since I'm not performing abortions. I'm just doing my job. At the same time, it felt like the days of chivalry. There were a bunch of guys in the congregation who wanted to go outside and beat those people up, have them dragged off by the police. They were defending the castle and protecting the fair lady, which stirred a primitive feeling. That part was great.

Susan's experience with the picketers illustrates the mix of emotions that can be aroused when a complex situation carries with it feminist and possibly conflicting overtones. Here, the congregation expressed support for a bedrock feminist issue: a pregnant woman's right to choose. Its associate rector—a visible female role model—reacted well under pressure, expressing justifiable anger but keeping her cool.

On the other hand, Susan didn't deal directly with the picketers. Jim Adams, the male rector, went outside and invited them in, but they declined. If Jim had been the object of the picketing, one wonders whether Susan would have dealt with them—not because she might lack the courage (I'm sure she wouldn't), but because Jim may not have wished to be perceived as hiding behind his female subordinate's vestments. And when the male parishioners offered to drive off the picketers, Susan had a rescue fantasy—the fair lady protected by her knights. To an old sexist like me, Susan's fantasy was quite human and rather endearing, but perhaps not the reaction one would expect from a thoroughgoing feminist.

In the Noel group's second appearance at St. Mark's, their protest agenda was expanded to include our gay members and Jim Adams's support of gay issues. Karen Byrne recalled arriving early with her two small children to sing in the children's choir. The picketers were "alarmingly aggressive," telling the kids the church was a "house of sin," and that they should turn back.

The Noel people returned to St. Mark's on the anniversary of the Supreme Court's decision in *Roe v. Wade*. They placed leaflets on car windshields and carried placards listing the "ten most wanted" abortionists in the United States. Susan commented to me wryly, "My husband had the distinction of making the list."

My awareness of women's issues at St. Mark's was, for many years, limited and more intellectual than emotional. I had no idea of the intense feelings those issues stirred up until I took a Christian education class titled

"Me and My Sexuality." During the first class, the men and women were divided into two groups. One of the teachers read "the Rules," the product of a male chauvinist mentality, which sarcastically decreed:

> The female always makes the rules.
> The female has the right to be angry or upset at any time.
> The female is ready when she is ready.

Each group was then given a copy of the Rules. Its members were told to list those rules with which they agreed, and to write alternative rules where they disagreed.

We men weren't emotionally engaged by the exercise. Some of us found it hard to take seriously. But I was surprised to discover that several men, sometimes the majority, agreed with some of the Rules. The full class reassembled, and the men's group reported its consensus rules. A few of us dissented to parts of the report. I was embarrassed to be associated with a clutch of Neanderthals.

The women were angered and offended by the Rules. They spoke bluntly; several were, as they put it, "pissed off." The women proposed contrasting alternatives cutting in the opposite direction. I wasn't surprised by the feminist tenor of the women's alternatives, but I was taken aback by the vehemence with which they were expressed. Here was my restrained and reasonable friend Linda Ewald, blue eyes flashing and coming on like Gloria Steinem.

This Christian education exercise underlined how hard it is for someone with my sexist background to fully understand and sympathize with women's opinions and feelings about feminist issues. We men haven't suffered gender discrimination. Beyond that, we've been the discriminators—with the approval of our culture and, until the 1970s, with the acceptance, even collusion, of most women. My twenty-nine-year-old son grew up in the 1980s and developed more enlightened and sensitive attitudes than his father.

Feminist issues in a church like St. Mark's are often verbal—the way people talk to God and to each other. *The Book of Common Prayer* makes repeated reference to God as "Father." Some other references are clearly masculine, if less explicit—for example, "God of power and might." Most people seem to accept these references because they're imbedded in Christian tradition. My friend Karen Byrne ran for a Vestry seat one year. In her election speech, she suggested an amendment to the Lord's Prayer:

"Our Mother who art in heaven . . . " Her suggestion may have cost her the election.

Like the liturgy, the 1982 hymnal reflects an attempt at "gender neutrality" that, according to the compilers, "resulted in the sensitive alteration of texts which could be interpreted as either pejorative or discriminatory." While I sympathize with the compilers' objective, some of their "sensitive alterations" strike a false note. For example, when Isaac Watts wrote the majestic lyrics of his hymn "O God Our Help in Ages Past," he began the final verse with "Time, like an ever rolling stream, bears all its sons away." The compilers substituted "years" for "sons." (Perhaps they were tempted to add "and daughters" after "sons," but that would have spoiled the meter.) Rector Adams, in a rare lapse into pedantry, defends the compilers' change, arguing that the original language was intended to refer to the passage of time, not to the death of people. The text is ambiguous in that regard. Be that as it may, the change butchered Watts's poetry in the name of political correctness.

Karen Byrne doesn't shy away from feminist disputes—this one nonliturgical. When the wooden doors of the church were in disrepair, Karen was among the preservationists who questioned Rector Adams's proposal to substitute glass doors. One day, interested parishioners gathered at the doors to discuss the options, and Karen pointed to a weakness in the case for glass doors. Adams, who is about my age and, like me, a recovering sexist, responded with some acerbity, suggesting that Karen didn't understand his proposal. Adams added a brush-off to the put-down, calling Karen "sweetie."

Karen was furious, marched home muttering to herself, wrote Jim an indignant letter the next day, and hand-carried it to the church office. Following a prudent cooling-off period, Jim phoned Karen to apologize, noting that his daughters had faulted him for sexist language in the past and expressing the belief that this incident would underscore that message. Karen was satisfied with Jim's apology. In later years, although women at St. Mark's didn't think of Jim as a cutting-edge feminist, they applauded his increased sensitivities to women's issues.

Fifteen years at St. Mark's have brought real changes in my attitudes toward women, but from time to time I'm reminded of where I came from. In the spring of 1996, I watched the NCAA Tournament semifinal basketball game between the Lady Volunteers of Tennessee and the University of Connecticut Lady Huskies. The Lady Vols' point guard, Michelle Marciniak (twenty-one points, seven rebounds, six assists), reportedly takes the court with a picture of Michael Jordan stuffed in her sock. With the game on the line, Marciniak dribbled through three Husky defenders and took the ball straight to the hoop. "Awesome," I said to myself, "she plays just like a man."

Chapter 13

Gays and Lesbians at St. Mark's

If you do not tell the truth about yourself, you cannot tell it about other people.
　　　　　—Virginia Woolf, *The Moment and Other Essays*

$\mathcal{B}$ill Repsher celebrated his fiftieth birthday with a dance party at St. Mark's. David Showers, a gay man who came to St. Mark's with his partner, Bruce Calvin, didn't go to such affairs at first because he hadn't felt free to dance with Bruce. David ran into Bill when Bill was putting together a tape of his favorite dance music—the Rolling Stones ("I Can't Get No Satisfaction"), the Everly Brothers ("Wake Up Little Susie"). David told Bill that he would dance at his party if he would include "Raining Men," a disco song from the 1980s, on his tape. Bill did, and David danced with Bruce.

According to David, dancing is on the leading edge of evolving and sometimes ambiguous relationships between gay and lesbian members and the straight majority at St. Mark's. In other times and places, women dancing together may not have caused comment—at least when there weren't enough men to go around. That may still be true, for example, in Iowa, my home state. But in a major city with a large gay population and heightened awareness of sexual orientations, women dancing together would probably be interpreted as a sexual statement. It would take some courage for women—whether lesbian or straight—to dance together, even at St. Mark's. What about a gay man asking a straight man to dance? Or a straight woman asking a gay man to dance? Most of us would feel awkward, at least initially, in those situations. But a willingness to explore them can break down barriers between people.

John Lineberger, among the first openly gay men at St. Mark's, described dancing with Bill Jordan, who is straight:

> Karen Wooding said she would dance with me, but then she danced off with Bill Jordan. I went up to them and said to Karen, "Hey, I thought we were going to dance." Bill said okay but Karen walked away, so I gave Bill a joking shall-we-dance gesture. Later, Bill came up to me and said, "How about that dance now?" I no more wanted to dance with him than I wanted to swing from a chandelier, but I thought, "If he's got the courage to ask me, I've got to do it." Bill and I were dancing when Betsy Athey started dancing between us, not realizing that Bill and I were dancing together. Bill gave Betsy a gentle shove aside, and she looked at us as if to say, "Oh, well, it's St. Mark's. No big deal."

John and Bill both report that their dancing together was an ice breaker that led to a better relationship between them. It also indicates to John that "the congregation is being a little playful, and more accepting." David Showers agrees: "A lot of people who have been theoretically comfortable in dealing with gay people have moved to a more experiential level of dealing."

Washington, D.C., has a large gay population, a gay newspaper (the *Blade*), gay bars and restaurants, and favored residential areas—including Capitol Hill where St. Mark's is located. When I came to St. Mark's in 1982, gay members of the congregation weren't openly gay at the church (although they may have been with friends, family, or in other limited settings). I knew one lesbian couple whose relationship was openly acknowledged, but it must have been a lonely place for them. They eventually left Washington to operate a bed-and-breakfast in rural Pennsylvania.

During the late 1980s, gay members began to come out at St. Mark's. In 1991, Bill Landers became a candidate for the Vestry. In his election night speech, Bill revealed that he had tested HIV positive. I didn't vote for him, partly because his revelation came across to me as a bid for sympathy. But most of the congregation apparently didn't share my reaction, and Bill won a Vestry seat in a close race. He was unable to complete his term due to failing health, but he had broken new ground. Another gay man was elected to the Vestry in 1992 without, however, openly acknowledging his sexual orientation. I think most of us were under the impression that he was gay but didn't consider it significant. Bill Landers died of AIDS in 1994.

I first met John Lineberger in an otherwise forgettable Christian education class. One evening the class viewed a film of the Olympic games in
which two male Russian athletes kissed each other on the mouth. During
the comment period, I acknowledged that I had found the male kissing
scene hard to take. I was sitting next to John and realized after I had spoken that my comment probably sounded homophobic. So I offered a clari-
fying comment—that my discomfort may have come from fear of my own
gay side—which made me feel enlightened, honest, and brave.

Interviewing John for this book, I asked him what his reaction had
been at the time. He recalled mixed feelings. On the one hand: "Who is
this bastard coming at me with his problem? I don't want to hear that in
this class." At the same time, John felt that my statement "was very real,
very truthful. It made me realize that there are people at St. Mark's who
accept me, but who have difficulty with some things I represent. As much
as I do a disservice to myself to hide who I really am, I do a disservice to
others if I ask them to squelch authentic feelings about gay people."

John, thirty, grew up near Lancaster, Ohio, on Rural Route 3. He graduated from the Columbus College of Art and Design and moved to Washington, D.C., because he was "afraid to go to New York." Following a stint
as a freelance artist, he became art director for a national magazine.

While in Ohio, John had joined Integrity, a gay religious organization
that has chapters at the diocesan level across the country. Members have
their own worship services, get together socially, and are politically active
in the church. As a result of that experience, John came to think of the
Episcopal Church as welcoming to gays. In fact, St. Mark's has been opening its doors to gay organizations since the 1960s, when the Mattachine
Society of Washington held its first meetings there. However, Rector Bill
Baxter turned down the society's request for a gay-only Eucharist, believing
it would send a message of isolation.

When John came to Washington in 1987, he was looking for a church
that would be open to gays and have an active community life. Walking
past St. Mark's by chance, he saw a sign referring to the "St. Mark's Players,"
the "Dance Company," and the "Yoga Center." His curiosity aroused, John
attended a Sunday service on Pentecost, a day set aside to honor the Holy
Spirit. As John recalled: "Jim Adams told the congregation to take their red
balloons out of their Sunday bulletins and blow them up. Then he blessed
the balloons and told everyone to set forth the Holy Spirit into the world.

Red balloons were flying all over the place. I knew this was the place I wanted to be."*

But John wanted to assure himself that St. Mark's would accept gays and take them seriously. He made an appointment with Jim Adams and told him: "I don't want to be insulated in a totally gay community, in a subculture. I want to be challenged. I want to see what St. Mark's has to offer me, a gay man, in a wider community. But I need to know that this church will accept me. I'm not going to beat my head against a wall. I did that in Ohio and I'm not going to do that again."

John found the meeting reassuring, but only up to a point. He found disturbing Adams's statement that being gay or straight was not much talked about at St. Mark's. He read that to mean that gays were expected to keep their sexual orientations to themselves. That reading probably was an accurate reflection of the status of gays at St. Mark's in 1987.

John later came to think of Jim Adams as a strong advocate for the gay cause. In 1992, Jim testified before a congressional committee in support of "domestic partners" legislation, under which gay and lesbian employees of the city could earn city health benefits for their partners as well as themselves. Jim testified that the legislation would set a good example for children because it sends the message that "human beings are human beings." Congressman Clyde Holloway, a Louisiana Republican opposing the legislation, asked Jim if he were a homosexual. Jim replied: "I am not. Are you?" The congressman didn't respond.

John was a member of the last confirmation class teaching team led by Jim Adams before his retirement. He recalled that on the drive to Rehoboth, Delaware, for a class weekend, the team talked about the place of gays in the church. Jim Adams went over the biblical quotations sometimes applied out of context to gays and said they were all misinterpreted. Until that moment, John had always had a doubt in the back of his mind that he was acceptable to God. For the first time, he felt he was okay.

David Showers, forty-seven, is an ordained United Methodist minister who has served as pastor of several parishes and worked on the national level for the Methodist Church. David is divorced and has a college-age son. He met his partner, Bruce Calvin, while he was doing doctoral work and Bruce was completing his Master of Divinity degree at the Wesley Theological Seminary in Washington.

* The hand-blown balloons at Pentecost are not to be confused with the machine-blown, helium balloons at Easter (see chapter 14).

David and Bruce live on Capitol Hill and first came to St. Mark's by chance in 1986. They were attracted by the imaginative approach to liturgy and by the sharing of power between clergy and lay members. David and Bruce were up-front about their relationship from the beginning: "While we aren't what I call 'flag-flying faggots,' we were very clear that we were a couple, and that was how we were going to relate to the community." They had met Jim Adams and his wife, Ginny, at the nearby Folger Theater, where the four had season tickets. David recalls that when they came to St. Mark's, Ginny Adams "made a point, on a number of occasions, of talking to us and pointing things out." Others "didn't know how to react to us; they were squirmy and squeamish." David and Bruce were the first to list each other in the church phone directory as "spouse." Other gay couples have followed suit. After ten years, David reports that most people have "become comfortable enough with us so that they can ask the stupid question."

Both David and Bruce have taught several classes at St. Mark's. Before teaching the junior-high class at Sunday school, David told the Christian education directors: "I need to be crystal clear with you before I start teaching kids. I'm a gay man. If there's going to be a problem with parents, let's think about that now." The directors replied: "It's not an issue. If there's a problem, send them to us." The issue never arose.

Unlike gay men, lesbians at St. Mark's maintain a low profile. As Pat Latin, a lesbian parishioner, told me, "We don't even know each other." Pat, fifty-six, is from Akron, Ohio. She has an M.A. in American literature and has taught college English, but her interests and abilities extend beyond the classroom. In her day job with a military contractor, Pat is a technical editor and writer. As a freelancer, she writes about women, travel, and fishing.

Pat is divorced and has no children. For twelve years during her marriage—and for awhile afterward—she was a professional performance and video artist. Her work, which she describes as "in the tradition of Duchamp and Claes Oldenburg," embraced media such as film, video, and slide dissolve to express psychologically linked images in a nonlinear narrative (you need to see it). Her works have been shown in galleries and museums in Washington, D.C., New York City, Antwerp, Belgium, and in many other cities here and abroad. She was a visiting lecturer in media art at the Corcoran School of Art for two years. When Pat had to go to work full-time, the demands of performance and media art, particularly travel, became too great; she switched to creating and exhibiting traditional drawings and nontraditional sculpture. Pat is president of the Lion's Share Investment Club at St. Mark's and is considering working as an investment adviser for a nonprofit organization after she retires.

Pat was a cradle Episcopalian and, after years of not attending church, came to St. Mark's in 1982 to reexamine her values through confirmation class and to return to a guided spirituality. After coming to St. Mark's, Pat went through a transition from "living as a heterosexual to living my life as a lesbian." During that period, she was dating a man and a woman. She saw a movie, *Desert Hearts,* about a woman moving to Nevada in order to establish residency for a divorce. She meets a young woman, and they eventually become lovers. It was a realistic portrayal of transition. "I saw it many times, using it as a mantra for answers."

The transition was wrenching—like going to a foreign country and seeing directional signs in an unrecognizable alphabet. "I never found a satisfactory way of introducing this change to friends at church who had known me only as a divorced heterosexual person and who were, after my parents died, my only 'family.' It was equivalent to telling my parents. Eventually I came to realize that although my life had changed, I could be basically the same person I was before the transition—but I had shifted my emotional focus to women."

When Pat first came to St. Mark's, it wasn't a supportive place for gays and lesbians; that remained true until the late 1980s. When Pat took the confirmation class, she asked Jim Adams how the Episcopal Church treated homosexuals. As Pat recalled, Jim answered that they were tolerated. Pat found that answer unsettling, and it heightened her ambivalence about revealing something so private to her fellow parishioners without making them feel betrayed by her change. For a time after that, Pat came to church only occasionally. She noted that, over time, Jim Adams's attitude softened, but that she "didn't trust the change at first."

Pat talked about coming out selectively at church, at work, and elsewhere. At St. Mark's, she doesn't withhold the fact that she is a lesbian if that information is relevant—for example, in a Christian education class. Unlike some gay men, Pat hasn't adopted a public posture at St. Mark's as a lesbian, but she finds the idea of bringing her partner to the spring dance "intriguing." She is out at work and to most of her friends, but not to those who she feels might be upset by her changed identity. "It's a never-ending process, and it never gets any easier."

Pat does talk freely about her participation in an Episcopal lesbian group whose membership comes from the entire Washington metropolitan area and from as far away as North Carolina and New York. This organization gives its members a unique opportunity to share experiences and worship together with other lesbians of faith. She has written, published, and signed articles about spirituality from a lesbian standpoint because it's important to stand up for the right to worship and be accepted in a traditional church. "I have never doubted that I and all homosexual people are children of God. We are another thread of the diverse human fabric and are always accepted in God's sight."

Gays and lesbians are subject to external pressures from living in a church community where they make some people uncomfortable, even though nothing is said. Largely as a result of those pressures, they also have to struggle with internal conflicts flowing from their occasional paranoid interpretations of straight members' innocent words or actions. David Showers recalled his own paranoid reaction involving the "intinction cup"—a cup of wine into which a member receiving communion can choose to dip the consecrated bread instead of drinking wine from the common cup: "It seemed to me that there was one person who, every time he stood beside *me* for communion, would always take the intinction cup because he didn't want to drink out of the common cup after me. To this day, I don't know if that was his reason. I had to get past that and say, 'It doesn't matter.'"

Gay and lesbians at St. Mark's have formed the Lavender Lions, a social group that gets together several times a year. The organizers picked the name because they thought it was funny, but when the Lions' formation was announced from the pulpit one Sunday by Bruce Calvin, the joke fell flat on the majority-straight congregation. John Lineberger recalled that "people had no idea that 'Lavender Lions' was tongue-in-cheek, that it was okay for them to laugh." John describes the Lions as providing an opportunity for people "just to be who they are, a place to figure out how they want to present themselves to the congregation." Beyond that, the very existence of a gay organization has helped to promote acceptance of gays in all aspects of church life.

Being gay or lesbian is difficult. Even in a supportive place like St. Mark's, some courage is required. John Lineberger stated his bottom line: "Who would choose to live a life of oppression and abuse? But I was made this way. This is the way I am. And I'll live into that life completely."

In recent years, ordination of gay men and lesbians as priests has been among the most contentious issues in the national Episcopal Church. The issue came to a head when Bishop Walter Righter, then an assistant to Bishop John Spong in the Diocese of Newark, New Jersey, was charged with heresy for ordaining a gay man in an open relationship. (Of course, gays have long been ordained as priests and ministers in various denominations, if they were willing to stay in the closet.) After a contentious canonical trial, Righter was acquitted in 1996. A serious, sometimes impassioned, debate continues within the national Church, but the Righter case didn't evoke much comment at St. Mark's. To me it was reminiscent of the Scopes trial—something out of another time.

Chapter 14

Community Life

Bring hither the fatted calf and kill it;
and let us eat and be merry.

—Luke 15:23

*M*y biggest disappointment in fifteen years at St. Mark's is never being named Crab of the Year. I haven't even been nominated, despite the fact that my record as a curmudgeon is superior to the records of those who have been thus honored. Take Margaret Hilton, for example. As chair of the Worship Committee, Hilton led the charge against helium balloons at Easter services, contending they might float east from St. Mark's, lose buoyancy over the ocean, and be eaten by sea turtles who would choke on the rubber and die. Crabby, yes, but hardly deserving of the highest honor.

The case for Bruce Calvin, last year's crab, was even weaker. Calvin had been complaining to everyone who would listen that we need more "categories"—those cryptic descriptions of mind and spirit concocted by Christian education guru Charles Penniman for people who seek wisdom in obscurity. A true crab's painful duty is to expose folly, not perpetuate it. Yet lightweights like Hilton and Calvin are raised up while I—the Vestry member who voted against a baby-sitter for the nursery and called for full disclosure of the rector's compensation—am ignored. It's unfair and un-Christian.

The Crab of the Year award is conferred by the College of Crustaceans. The college is the creation of the Committee to Have More Fun, which was founded by Bart Barnes, an obituary writer for the *Washington Post*. The college sponsors an annual Fourth-of-July Crabfeast, held sometime in August. After gorging on hot crabs, cold beer, corn-on-the-cob, and watermelon, that year's crab is crowned, gives a short, crabby acceptance speech (I liked Crane Miller's "It's about time"), and reigns until a successor is named.

Bart outlined the process and standards for selecting the Crab of the Year: "The crab is chosen at the annual dinner of the College of Crustaceans. The award is made for either a single act of crabbiness during the preceding year or for a pattern of crabby behavior. The award is made in good fun, and only those we love are considered." I meet those standards—except perhaps for the love part. I suspect the process is rigged.

Baptists and Seventh-Day Adventists frown on dancing as a step down the slippery slope to perdition. At St. Mark's, we clear away the chairs and dance in the nave of the church. Just plain fun, unadulterated with any religious justification. The fall dinner dance and the Mardi Gras ball are relatively formal affairs—by reservation only, black tie optional. Music from a live band includes standards like "Stardust"—for bad dancers like me—and full-volume rock 'n' roll. The food is excellent, the wine is acceptable, and the beer is microbrewery. Tickets might cost twenty dollars—pricey for an evening at church, but only half the cost of an upscale restaurant meal in Washington.

Dancing and fund-raising are sometimes combined. The focus of our companion relationship with the San Marcos cluster of congregations in Honduras is a summer trip by St. Mark's teens and adult leaders to work on needed projects. (Chapter 16 describes my trip to Honduras with a St. Mark's group in 1996.) Most of those who make the trip pay their own way, but money is needed for scholarships and project expenses.

Every spring, the Honduras Committee puts on a "Wake Up the Earth" fund-raiser—so named because the environment is a banner to which (witness the helium balloons) many at St. Mark's will rally. This festive affair features south-of-the-border cuisine, all the *cerveza* you can drink, live music with a Latin beat, a silent auction, and, if the Spirit is moving among us, a live auction of anything that isn't nailed down. One year, Eric Dannenmaier, a leader in our Honduran activities, auctioned off a day with his dog Arlo for twenty-five dollars.

When I signed up for the 1996 trip to Honduras, I automatically became a member of the production crew for the fund-raising dance. Typical of such enterprises, an enormous amount of time was devoted by many people to scores of mindless tasks. The nave of the church had to be made to resemble a village square in a Latin American country. This required colorful, crepe-paper banners, scissored in random geometries and hung eight feet above the dance floor (for intimacy). I specialized in cutting palm fronds from two shades of green construction paper. My fronds framed the entrance and dangled from the supporting posts in the nave, lending verisimilitude to the construction-paper coconuts and banana bunches.

The night before the dance, our crew cleared the floor of the nave—moving two hundred chairs and kneelers, the altar, and other paraphernalia of worship. The altar platforms were a challenge—cumbersome bulks which, on other than holy ground, might cause a hernia. It took three of us to push and drag each platform into the library. When we went back on Friday afternoon to finish decorating, the altar platforms were back in the middle of the nave because two wedding rehearsals had been scheduled for that same afternoon. Apparently Rector Adams is incapable of doing a wedding walk-through unless he's standing eight inches above the prospective bride and groom. The weddings rehearsed, we muscled the altar platforms back into the library, like Sisyphus pushing his boulder. After that, I retreated to the kitchen to slice avocados.

The festivities were supposed to begin at 6:30, but it was after 7:00 before people began to trickle in. We had seats for one hundred in the parish hall, which we had planned to use in shifts, but there were still a lot of empty seats at 7:30. What would we do with a mountain of chicken burritos which—submerged in a spicy sauce—we were passing off as enchiladas? The hired band struck up a tune about 8:00 and one or two couples ventured onto the dance floor. But there weren't enough people on hand for a critical mass.

Our hopes for a net profit hung on the silent auction. About one hundred items were laid out on tables, with minimum bids for each. There was some interesting imported stuff—jewelry, ceramics, shawls—at reasonable prices, and a lot of two-dollar junk. In years past, we had done well auctioning off weeks or weekends at vacation homes, but only one owner had felt that philanthropic this year.

I had been asked to bring an auction item from home. I wasn't willing to donate one of my daughter's paintings. I considered, but decided against, contributing the 1890 model, 7.6-millimeter Mauser my dentist father had mysteriously acquired during World War II. Some of the timider souls might think a German infantry rifle in working order unsuitable for a church auction. So I volunteered to write a poem to the buyer's specifications, with a five-dollar minimum bid for a bad poem and a fifty-dollar minimum for a good one.

Kathryn Chefetz bought a bad poem for the five-dollar minimum. I can churn out bad poetry like a butcher grinds hamburger. For Kathryn, I produced "Oh Honduras," which begins:

> Oh Honduras, land where our hearts bleed.
> Where we reach out to our fellow person
> So his life will get better, instead of worsen.

Eileen Blumenthal bid twenty-five dollars for a good poem—only half the minimum bid. Not wishing to turn away money but sensitive to standards issues, I wrote Eileen a mediocre poem. "Honduras, Mon Amour" begins like this:

> Let us go then, time to mosey
> Me and you and David and Josie
> To the place where *ninos*, dawn to dark,
> Watch the *gringos* from St. Mark's.

A handful of revelers danced the last dance about 11:00. We put the decorations in a basement closet—to adorn another day—and dragged the altar platforms back into position. The 1996 "Wake Up the Earth" festival netted $1,500—a financial disappointment but not a total flop. In hindsight, veterans of earlier festivals believed there had been too many recent ticketed affairs at St. Mark's, particularly on Friday nights. Or it could have been that we had gone to the same well once too often. After eight consecutive years of waking up the earth, people were ready for a nap.

 Much of St. Mark's community life takes place off campus. I already mentioned Shrine Mont, the annual parish retreat in the Blue Ridge Mountains, from a program standpoint. Program aside, the rest of Shrine Mont is a busy, two-day exercise in community living and playing. About half the congregation and their young children usually attend. Most people rent a room in one of the cabins, but a sizable contingent, including me, camps out. Last year, a rainstorm dumped four inches of water into my old-fashioned tent on the first night. I stole away to a cabin, but, fearful of tarnishing my reputation as an outdoorsman, I returned to the campsite for meals as if nothing had happened.

Shrine Mont Saturday afternoon is for fun—swimming, volleyball, badminton, softball, tennis, or just sitting under a tree with a friend or a good book. Bob Hahn, a retired teacher and veteran bird-watcher, always takes a group birding. Through his seventies, Bowdie Craighill brought his boomerangs and offered lessons in that ancient skill. Scores of boys between the ages of nine and thirteen took Bowdie up on his offer, but no one was ever injured.

Saturday before supper, the traditional "Senior Warden's Cocktail Party" is held outdoors. Beer, wine, and soft drinks are furnished, but you have to bring your own martini. The senior warden gets the credit and doesn't have to pay for the drinks. Saturday after supper, and after the program session is out of the way, there's the traditional square dance, featuring Bob Dulcimer (his real name) as caller. Square is one way I can dance without injuring others—even a klutz can do-si-do.

Skeptic though I am, my sense of community at Shrine Mont peaks during the Sunday morning service, held on a tree-covered hillside with a rock grotto for the altar. Just being outdoors in dazzling sunshine is part of it. The heightened feeling of community is present, I think, because we've all left the city and gone away for a weekend devoted to one another. There's a brief sermon, communion, and the service usually closes with "Amazing Grace."

After the customary lunch of fried chicken, rice, and gravy, everybody goes home. Over the years, one gains a sense of tradition about the Shrine Mont weekend. I've been to all but one of the last fifteen—missing only to attend my son's college graduation.

People who become deeply involved in St. Mark's find their social lives closely linked to those they know from the church. This is partly because it's so hard to make friends as a newcomer in a big city and so easy at St. Mark's—provided one goes beyond the Sunday morning service and is at least moderately likable.

Some social activities are organized from the church but happen elsewhere. The Outsiders organize camping, canoeing, white-water rafting, and hiking outings for adults and kids looking for adventure, weenie roasts, and campfire singing. The Sailors of the Winged Lion do their thing on the Chesapeake Bay. There is a singles group for people in their twenties and thirties, which does the things that singles of that age do. Some of them eventually get married.

Birthdays, particularly milestones like forty or fifty, are a good excuse for a party. My family put together a backyard barbecue for me and my St. Mark's friends on my fiftieth birthday. Bob and Linda Ewald gave me a black T-shirt inscribed "Somewhere between Forty and Death."

Collie Agle celebrated fifty on a grander scale. Along with his invitations, he sent a lengthy excerpt from T. S. Eliot's *Four Quartets*. We were asked to write a reflection on where we found ourselves in midlife and to bring it to the party. Thinking Eliot would stimulate plenty of solemnity in the other guests, I wrote a parody of several Eliot poems: "The Love Song of J. Alfred Prufrock," "Gerontion," *The Waste Land*, "The Hollow Men," "Sweeny among the Nightingales." My effort was well received.

The arts are important to community life at St. Mark's. The St. Mark's Players put on three productions each year. In the 1995–1996 season, the Players presented *Quilters, Amadeus*, and *West Side Story*, which received an enthusiastic review in the *Washington Post*. Casts are a combination of St. Mark's members and outside talent. St. Mark's members attend in numbers but the Players' reputation draws theatergoers from throughout the Washington area. Most performances are sold out.

The music program, once a weakness, has become a strength under Keith Reas, music director since 1991. Keith is a graduate of the Oberlin College Conservatory of Music, the University of Oregon, and the Eastman School of Music. He is a concert-level organist and a talented director of choirs. Under Keith's direction, the choirs of St. Mark's have annually presented major works with orchestra, including an acclaimed Mozart *Requiem*. In the summer of 1996, they sang on tour in English cathedrals and parish churches. In addition to service music, the church presents a concert series by outstanding artists each year. St. Mark's recently revived children's choir program is growing, as is its music studio, which offers private instruction in piano, flute, violin, cello, organ, and voice.

Visual artists—painters, sculptors, and photographers—have become active in the church under the leadership of Penny Farley; John Lineberger, art director of a national magazine; David Evelyn, a high school art teacher; and Betty Foster, a potter and sculptor. The halls under the nave have become gallery space, with members' pieces on display and for sale. John, David, and Betty taught a class, "Drawing on the Spirit," that was designed for art skeptics. The idea was to bring in people who think they have no artistic talent and to help them discover that they do. I went to the first couple of sessions before concluding, once again, that I'm hopeless. During the first class we students, working together, created a single, abstract painting. I distinguished myself by spilling a pot of paint on the carpet.

The St. Mark's Dance Studio, housed above the parish hall, has been a center of ballet, modern and liturgical dance since the 1960s. The Dance

Company and Studio are described in chapter 18, along with their founder and director, Mary Craighill.

St. Mark's is a full-service church. Therapists from the Pastoral Counseling and Consultation Center see clients in the classrooms on weekdays. Votaries of yoga assume the classical positions on weeknights.

Community life revolves largely around the activities that bring people together. Those of us seeking new relationships participate in activities not for their own sake but for the chance to meet and get to know other people. In a church of some seven hundred adults, after fifteen active years I know about two hundred by name, have some relationship with perhaps fifty, and count about a dozen as friends. I consider myself fortunate. Whenever I begin to think about moving somewhere else, maybe Boston or Baltimore, I think about what I've built over the years at St. Mark's and dismiss the idea.

Relationships among people in the St. Mark's community have a special quality of directness and candor not found in everyday life. When people become church members, they promise before the congregation that (among other things) they will express their concerns and complaints directly to the person involved. In my experience, this demanding standard of behavior is met to a remarkable degree. We saw some examples in earlier chapters. When the rector spoke to her in sexist terms, Karen Byrne called him on it. When Buzz March emasculated my John Donne reading, I let him know how I felt. Of course, it can be painful and awkward to confront another person with a mistake or a thoughtless action. All of us are aware of this, and we let a lot of things pass (or complain to our friends behind the offender's back). But the existence of a standard requiring directness and candor does promote greater honesty and openness in the community.

Chapter 15

Spirituality

I like the silent church before the service begins, better than any preaching.
—Ralph Waldo Emerson, *Self-Reliance*

Michael really likes the community aspect of basketball. He likes doing stuff with males. That's spiritual—what joins us together as human beings.
—Phil Jackson, head coach, Chicago Bulls, "The Running of the Bulls," *Sports Illustrated*

I have no living sense of commerce with a God. I envy those who have, for I know that the addition of such a sense would help me greatly.
—William James, *The Varieties of Religious Experience*

Some people at St. Mark's talk about spirituality as if it were a clearly defined concept. Statements like "I'm a spiritual person" and "I had a spiritual experience" are uttered as if everyone knows what they mean. I didn't know what spirituality means (I still don't), so I asked Rector Jim Adams to explain.

Adams finds spirituality "one of the most peculiar words in religious language today." He adds, "I never know what people are talking about unless I sit down and have them tell me a few stories about what they think is spiritual." Adams expressed puzzlement, for example, about an increasing interest among today's seminarians in being "spiritual." When asked, some of them will say they mean having a "spiritual director." They see someone—a sort of mentor or guru—periodically for "spiritual direction."

Seeking more help from the clergy, I took my question to Associate Rector Susan Gresinger. Susan doesn't know what "spirituality" means either, as the word is bandied about in churches. She "gets nervous around people who think of spirituality as some kind of overt activity—okay, now we're going to be spiritual." Susan associates spirituality with depth in ordinary experience—what she calls the "spiritual dimension"—sometimes found in personal relationships at their best, in an intimate relationship with another person, or in a community. She finds that dimension from time to time in the St. Mark's community when people reach out to one another in difficult times, for example, in the community's responses to terminal illness. Still no definition, but the example was helpful.

There does seem to be a consensus on one thing: spirituality is a good thing, something we could all use more of. Beyond that, we might approach a definition—or at least a clearer idea—from looking at different contexts in which the word is used.

Spirituality is often associated with ritual, prayer, or contemplation— God-focused activity. For example, when people kneel in solitary prayer after receiving communion, they are "being spiritual." There are those who complain that St. Mark's is too busy and noisy, that it "isn't spiritual enough." Many of these people participate in a contemplative prayer group or in a laying-on-of-hands ritual—available to those who want it—on the first Sunday of the month.

Some evangelical churches claim that rituals like the laying on of hands can cause the blind to see and the crippled to walk. The laying on of hands at St. Mark's isn't expected to work miracles—no crutches are cast aside— but, reportedly, it does make people feel better. We also have a foot-washing ritual on Maundy Thursday, just before Easter, in which even skeptics like me participate. Some describe foot washing as "spiritual." I can't say that I've been transported by the experience, but there is something about people washing each other's feet in a darkened church that evokes a sense of community.

Ann Craig lives a couple of blocks from the Washington National Cathedral. A veteran teacher and supervisor in the Christian education program, Ann spoke of an experience she thought of as spiritual. She had been supervising several coteachers who had battled one another to stalemate. Ann was in despair. Recalling the situation later, she observed: "When you get to the point where despair in your life is overwhelming, our culture offers escape—a drink, a movie, a therapist. Instead, you can look into despair directly." Ann remembered standing in her bedroom before going to a supervision meeting, looking out the window at the nearby cathedral, and saying, "Oh god, what am I going to do?" She had said those words before, but that was the first time she had meant them. And it helped.

After St. Mark's, what better place to seek the meaning of spirituality than the Harvard Divinity School? Ari Goldman, a Jew and formerly religion correspondent for the *New York Times*, spent a sabbatical year at Harvard's "Div School" to deepen his understanding of other religions. Goldman later chronicled his experience in a book, *The Search for God at Harvard*. In a chapter on spirituality, Goldman describes several varieties of experience, starting with his own: "Spirituality for me is the sum total of all the acts of my day, waking with a prayer, eating kosher, sharing with my friends, even, in my mother's constellation, taking out the garbage. Judaism makes everything holy, ties me back to history, *and connects me with the spirit of God*." (Italics mine.)

Goldman goes on to describe other kinds of spirituality, as related to him by his classmates. Linda, an Anglican from Canada, found spirituality at Harvard "in the connections between people," especially "among older women at the Div School who, like her, had returned to study after raising a family." Ann, a Unitarian classmate and a linguist, found her spirituality in words. For her, "seeing God as a verb was really helpful." Robert, a middle-aged Episcopalian and businessman-turned-theology-student, found spirituality everywhere—"in the classroom, in the library, in the chapel, in the faculty, and in his fellow students."

Goldman's examples have little to do with churches or prayer—the consciously God-centered activity we looked at first. The spirituality he found at the Harvard Divinity School was individualized, growing out of each person's faith, upbringing, education, and other life experiences. God is wherever you find Him, and everywhere to be found. Indeed, spirituality for Goldman can include taking out the garbage for his mother.

There are, however, a few consistent threads. According to Goldman, spirituality involves transcending the everyday world and, in some way, experiencing God. Such experiences are subjective—one doesn't actually *see* God—and primarily emotional rather than intellectual. My survey of religious beliefs at St. Mark's (chapter 7) asked whether the member had experienced God, and if so, what that experience had been like. About 90 percent of survey respondents acknowledged having had such experiences. Here's a sampling of their descriptions:

- I have always had the sense since I was a child that God is real and that He hears me. It's hard to explain. It is like a warmth inside, a knowledge that something is.

- Whenever I see a mountain laurel blossom, or a seashell, or a baby's fingernail.
- In a sense of well-being and of being cared for even when bad things happen.
- In silent moments, alone and with others.
- As I fight prostate cancer.
- In my daily living—in joy, in sorrow, in remembrance, in work, in nature, in my child.

In these examples, God is involved, but—as in Goldman's Harvard examples—He appears in many different forms and places, not just in church or prayer. Broadening the concept of spirituality even further, some who hold themselves out as authorities on spirituality apparently don't even consider God an essential element. Wade Clark Roof, a sociologist and leading commentator on religion in the United States, offered this definition:

> By spirituality, I mean something deeply personal arising out of a person's experience and inner life. In its truest sense, spirituality gives expression to the being that is within us. It has to do with feelings, with the power that comes from within, with knowing our deepest selves. But it is also more than that. Spirituality reaches outward as well. If it has only to do with the inner life, then it's simply narcissism. But genuine spirituality reaches out to relationships, to people, to animals, to the environment. It has to do with the unity of experience.

For Roof, spirituality includes animals, relationships, the environment—everything but God and the kitchen sink. I find his murky definition somewhat less useful than a recipe for meatloaf. Besides, when someone starts talking about "the unity of experience," I start counting the spoons.

I don't mean to suggest that experiences that seem to fall only within Roof's expansive definition aren't worthwhile and perhaps religious in some sense. An enormous net, however unwieldy, is bound to catch a few fish. Ken Lee, a former senior warden at St. Mark's, provided an example from an experience of his while sailing:

> I inherited $40,000 when my father died. I bought a boat—my father's ongoing legacy to me. I'll be out on the Atlantic in the middle of the night, Sandy's [Ken's wife] down below. My father will be in my mind and heart, and I'll have a conversation with him—out loud. I want him to understand what I'm doing with the gifts he gave, even the

negative gifts. I wish he were still here so I could show him how I'm doing. Now, you can put all this in psychological terms—Psych 101. Do I have the sense that I'm in the presence of something spiritual and religious? Yes. Can I explain that? No.

Can a skeptic have a spiritual experience? Can an elephant fly or a horse sing the "Star Spangled Banner"? If, as believers like Goldman understand the concept, a spiritual experience necessarily involves some kind of transcendent connection with God, spiritual experience by a skeptic is a contradiction in terms—the skeptic has no God to connect with.

Skeptics like me believe in science and a material, predictable view of the world. As I tried to explain near the beginning of this book, as far as I'm concerned, if I can't see it, hear it, or touch it, it doesn't exist. My mind isn't open to the idea that an unseeable, unknowable God is somehow responsible for a spectacular sunset or a mountain laurel blossom. On the contrary, it seems to me that so-called spiritual experiences usually involve the recognized psychological phenomenon of projection—mistakenly attributing a reality outside oneself (God) to one's inner feelings, as in: "This symphony [sunset, theology lecture] is so moving [beautiful, brilliant] it must come from God."

It's not that I have no aesthetic appreciation of sunsets. But if I go beyond aesthetics to ask how sunsets happen, science supplies an answer—complete enough for me—in the relative alignments of the Earth and the Sun and in the ways clouds refract and reflect light waves. I don't need God to explain sunsets or, in theory, anything else.

And yet. One evening about ten years ago at the end of a tedious workday, I walked out of my government office toward the elevator. I hadn't done anything useful for days; I was feeling frustrated, depressed, and sorry for myself. As I stood waiting, the elevator doors opened and a pretty young girl, perhaps fourteen, emerged in a wheelchair. She deftly negotiated two sharp turns, then wheeled rapidly down the hall toward the office of one of my colleagues. I was struck by the expression on her young face—neither smiling nor frowning, just calmly doing what she needed to do. As I imagined it, she was content with her life, accepting she would spend it in a wheelchair.

Going down in the elevator, I suddenly felt ashamed. Here was a man of fifty who could walk, run, and even dance a little feeling sorry for himself, while a kid in a wheelchair was gamely playing the hard hand life had dealt her. As I walked home, I began to feel better, holding my head erect and squaring my shoulders. Later on, I wondered about the seeming coincidence of the crippled girl crossing my path just when I needed her.

I would have continued to dismiss that incident as a coincidence except that similar things have happened to me since—perhaps too often for coincidence. Just when I'm allowing myself the luxury of depression, someone in a wheelchair appears, like a guardian angel. Tom Foggin, who runs the book stall at St. Mark's, maintains that incidents that appear to be coincidence are really God at work in the world. I lean toward a more prosaic explanation of my angels: there are always a lot of handicapped people around; it's just that I notice them more when *I'm* feeling handicapped.

Serendipitous events aren't enough to shake my deeply rooted belief in a lawful world with, theoretically, an explanation for everything. Even if there is no ready explanation from the laws of chemistry and physics, it's a long leap indeed from a minor, seemingly mysterious occurrence to a "God of power and might" (as the Episcopal liturgy describes Him). Still, I have to admit that such events suggest that something not dreamt of in my philosophy may be abroad in the world.

From time to time, I've had experiences at St. Mark's that I don't call "spiritual" because, in William James's apt phrase, they don't give me a "living sense of commerce with God." But they do include elements often associated with experiences others might call spiritual. They seem to occur most often for me when the congregation is singing hymns. The fourth verse of John Newton's "Amazing Grace" goes like this:

Through many dangers, toils, and snares
I have already come;
'Tis grace that brought me safe thus far,
And grace will lead me home.

When I sing these words with the other members of the congregation, I sometimes experience a surge of emotions, which, at least for a few moments, lifts me out of myself. I stop obsessing about the pedestrian details of my daily life. I think instead about the "toils and snares" I've gotten through—serious illness, job loss, divorce—and I know I'm with others who have suffered the same, and worse. I feel a kinship with my fellow survivors—a transcendent feeling, if you will—and a shared longing for grace, for someone to lead me home. In those moments, it doesn't matter that I don't believe in divine grace.

The stirring, militant strains of the "Battle Hymn of the Republic" evoke very different but equally valuable feelings. As a 1960s civil rights lawyer, I associate the "Battle Hymn" with Selma, with working late at the Justice Department, and with Bobby Kennedy's funeral. Truth "marching on" is an evocative theme that, like "Amazing Grace," fosters a sense of solidarity with those around me and people I once worked with for a cause. Hymns like these must touch chords in anyone raised in the Christian tradition.

My reactions to hymns are heavily emotional—reactions which might not occur without the backdrops of organ music and stained glass. Can one have a spiritual experience grounded in the intellect rather than the emotions? That might open up new possibilities for skeptics with an analytical bent. Jim Adams thinks so: "Many people associate spirituality with emotions. It gives them a feeling of comfort which they would call spiritual. I equate thinking with spirituality, since my training and personality lead me to value thinking more highly than other human processes." There are times at St. Mark's when I have a predominantly intellectual experience that seems to have a spiritual element in the sense in which Adams was using it. Perhaps the best example is the Confession of Sin in the Sunday service. This is the one time during the week when I deliberately step back from myself, look inward, reflect on what I've done, right and wrong, and what I've left undone. Having thought about those things, I sometimes take steps to atone.

These are some thoughts about spirituality from a decidedly unspiritual person. My view of the world, emphasizing science and measurable reality, means that I'm not open to some experiences that less skeptical people may find real and uplifting. Although I question the objective reality of some spiritual experiences (for example, those allegedly involving divine intervention), I don't question the sincerity of those who report them or the value of the experience to the reporter. Even skeptical people can experience valuable feelings and thoughts—some might call them spiritual—in a church. That's one of the reasons I go to St. Mark's.

Chapter 16

My Brother's Keeper

Charity suffereth long and is kind; charity envieth not; charity vaunteth not itself, is not puffed up.

I Corinthians 13:4

"Outreach" is the current term for church-based charity—from traditional activities like soup kitchens and used clothing drives to ongoing relationships between churches and poor communities. When I came to St. Mark's in 1982, there wasn't much interest in outreach. We didn't (still don't) run a soup kitchen. Only token amounts of money were being allocated to outreach, except indirectly through assessments to the Diocese of Washington, which engages in various charitable activities. A handful of members were active through Community Concerns, the St. Mark's outreach committee, distributing old clothes and dicing vegetables in a soup kitchen operated by another church.

Those of us who weren't involved in outreach in those days—the over-whelming majority of the congregation—had a rationale for not doing hands-on Christianity. We came to church (we said) to be "empowered," a buzzword from the St. Mark's mission statement connoting a state of readiness to do (unspecified) good. Having recharged our spiritual batteries, we would be prepared—in the words of the closing prayer in the Sunday service—"to go forth into the world to do the work that You have given us to do." The emphasis was on self-examination and personal growth (inward-looking activities) instead of what was happening in the streets. The theory had it that, empowered by Sunday services and Christian education classes, we would go forth to do good in our jobs and in our neighborhoods—good which would somehow, eventually, benefit the needy. A spiritual variant of "trickle down" economics, the theory also provided a convenient excuse for not getting one's hands dirty.

In the late 1980s, an infusion of energetic young people (in their twenties and thirties) arrived at St. Mark's. Not satisfied with study and prayer, they began to press for new programs and money for outreach. St. Mark's teenagers and young adults volunteered to work with the Salvation Army's Grate Patrol—a mobile soup kitchen and provider of blankets and used clothes to the homeless who congregate around warm-air grates on cold winter days in the District. Other volunteers took inner-city kids on monthly outings to places like Rock Creek Park, an apple orchard in Virginia, or the Luray Caverns. The new spirit of outreach proved contagious. I emerged from the contemplative life to help a "Christmas in April" team repair, clean, and paint a dilapidated ghetto house one Saturday. Zealous amateurs, we broke some crockery in the process but left the place in better shape than we found it.

Outreach came of age at St. Mark's during the 1989–1990 fund-raising drive to renovate the church. The Community Concerns people argued that we couldn't in good conscience spend $1.5 million on our building unless we were also prepared to spend some real money on the poor. They pressed the Vestry to allocate 5 percent of the funds raised for the renovation (about $75,000) to outreach. I was a member of the Vestry at the time. We were concerned that we wouldn't have enough money for the renovation, but we didn't want to close the door on the poor. We compromised and voted to allocate 3 percent of the total raised—still a substantial amount—to outreach.

One of the most ambitious and popular outreach initiatives at St. Mark's has grown out of a companion relationship formed in 1989 with four small Episcopal churches on the north coast of Honduras, known at St. Mark's as the "San Marcos cluster." Collie Agle, a former Peace Corps volunteer in Latin America and the principal architect of the relationship, has described it as "a mutuality of needs: we had something to give them, and they might have something to give us, if we let it happen." From the beginning, the San Marcos relationship was seen as an opportunity for St. Mark's teenagers to learn firsthand about another culture, a different language, and levels of poverty our kids hadn't seen at home. Teen groups from St. Mark's, accompanied by adult leaders, have gone to Honduras almost every summer since 1990 to work on projects through local schools and churches.

Honduras—bordered on the west by Guatemala, on the south by El Salvador, on the south and east by Nicaragua, and on the north by the Caribbean—is about the size of Pennsylvania. Parts of the country are spectacularly beautiful. The villages of the north coast are nestled between the Caribbean and, only a mile or two inland, mountains formed from volcanoes and later blanketed with lush vegetation and thick forests. A few fertile valleys and the coastal plain support plantations growing pineapples, bananas, and oil and coconut palms. Honduras was the prototypical "banana republic"—effectively controlled by the United Fruit Company—until other countries became the principal banana producers. The Dole pineapple logo is a familiar sight today on refrigerated semitrailer trucks headed for port.

Despite its primitive beauty and pockets of wealth, Honduras is one of the poorest countries in the Western Hemisphere. A few statistics: The unemployment rate hovers near 50 percent. The fortunate Honduran who has a job earns, on average, the equivalent of $1,000 per year. Washington, D.C., has 8,000 hospital beds for its population of 600,000; Honduras has 6,000 hospital beds for its population of 5 million. In the United States, a national average of 10 babies die for every 1,000 born—a 1 percent mortality rate. In Honduras, the infant mortality rate is more than five times as high—exceeding 50 deaths per 1,000 births. Honduras has the second-highest (after Haiti) rate of AIDS in the Western Hemisphere.

When I went to Honduras with a St. Mark's group in 1996, what I saw seemed to confirm that living conditions for most of the people were as bad as the statistics indicated. Outside the air terminal in San Pedro Sula, barefoot boys scarcely bigger than our duffel bags scrambled to be our porters. We had been forewarned about rampant theft and waved them off. Denied work, they turned to begging—hands out, lower lips protruding. The highway to the north coast is lined with typical homes for the country people—one or two small rooms, walls of cement block (some of sticks and mud), a corrugated tin roof or palm thatch, no running water or electricity.

North-coast towns like Puerto Cortés and Tela, lacking the redeeming natural beauty of the countryside, are dirty and depressing. Mangy stray dogs roam the streets, scavenging for food. The lottery—the only quick way out for the poor—does a brisk business. In Tela (former headquarters of the United Fruit Company), I counted three or four people selling lottery tickets on each block around the town square. Idlers in the square play checkers with bottle caps.

According to Father Antonio Carcel, an Episcopal priest in the north-coast town of Omoa with whom several St. Mark's groups had worked, violent street crime wasn't a serious problem in Honduras before the civil war in Nicaragua. There were many poor people—some of them desperate—but few guns to rob banks with. When the United States began providing weapons to the Nicaraguan Contras, however, neighboring Honduras became a major base and supply route. The eventual result: large numbers of weapons, including automatic weapons, appeared on the black market, and security became a major concern. It's now common practice for banks to station a private guard at the door, brandishing an assault rifle or a pistol-grip shotgun (known as a "street sweeper"). Despite such precautions, Father Carcel reports that robberies and shootings with U.S. weapons of war have become increasingly common in the towns and cities—something for Americans to atone for.

Some recent history explains why Episcopalians are to be found in remote villages of 98 percent Catholic Honduras. Hurricane Fifi, one of the most destructive in this century, swept across the north coast of Honduras in 1974, devastating villages and killing some two thousand people. Episcopal missionary priests joined the rebuilding effort, not only with their hands but also by bringing in money and technical assistance from the States. In response, entire villages along the north coast converted from Catholicism. By 1996, however, there were signs that the post-Fifi fervor for the Episcopal Church was cooling. The St. Mark's group of seven attended a Sunday service in Omoa in which they outnumbered the adult parishioners, all of whom were women. A Wednesday evening service at San Marcos produced a similar turnout.

An all-adult group—two men and five women—made the summer-of-1996 trip to Honduras. (A teen group had gone the previous year and another went in 1997, but there weren't enough interested and age-eligible kids in 1996.) Our leaders were David Whiteman ("Don Da-VEED" in Honduras) and Josie Jordan. David, a veteran of seven Honduras trips, is an economist with the Congressional Research Service, but his heart belongs to the outdoors. An expert in survival techniques, he showed us how to tie the "jug sling knot," a complex hitch he had invented to carry a two-liter plastic Coca Cola bottle full with water over one's shoulder while hiking, swatting mosquitoes, and wiping sweat from one's brow. When a rubber part of my new sandals broke, David fixed it with dental floss. He dispensed medicine for protesting bowels and demonstrated getting out of a hammock with dignity.

Josie Jordan, whom you met in chapter 4, had also been to Honduras before and was our principal planner, budgeter, and diplomat. The follow-ers—in addition to me—were Sondra Berger, a youth worker whose flu-ency in Spanish made her invaluable; Lindsay Lauder, a supervisor in a protected house for the mentally handicapped; Carole Sanford, a teacher of English as a second language; and Nadine Hathaway, a fund-raiser, musi-cian, and music teacher. At sixty-one, I was the oldest member of the group; Lindsay, twenty-five, was the youngest.

We left on an American Airlines flight from National Airport on June 22. After a stopover in Miami, we were greeted at the San Pedro Sula air-port by stifling heat (105 degrees, high humidity) and by the Episcopal bishop of Honduras, whose quiet word to a harried inspector got us through customs without having to wait for a baggage search.

We rented a ten-passenger Toyota van, stopped at a Texaco station for gas, and hit the road for the north coast, spirits and expectations high. About thirty kilometers down the road, the Toyota sputtered, gasped, and died. Off to a limping start. The engine failure was a mystery—the oil and water levels were up, and the tank was almost full of good Texaco gasoline. Three of us walked a mile to the nearest phone to call the rental agency. Two hours later, a second Toyota van arrived, identical to the first except that (as we learned at the next gas station) it had a "diesel fuel only" sticker on the fuel port.

We pressed on to Muchilena ("much wood" in Spanish), a north-coast village near San Marcos where St. Mark's groups have stayed before at an Episcopal conference center. The rooms and beds are comfortable, and the food, prepared by Rosa our Honduran cook, is quite good. It's a short walk into the village, where a *pulparia* (Honduran 7-Eleven) sells Honduran beer, Salva Vida, that is cold and cheap. Muchilena would be our base during the working part of the trip.

Our first morning in Honduras we met with Father Carcel, rector of Iglesia (church) Episcopal San Fernando Rey in nearby Omoa, to talk about projects we might tackle. (We had come with a list of possibilities but, lacking knowledge of local conditions and preferences, had to defer decisions.) Fa-ther Carcel knew exactly what he wanted us to do: help complete con-struction of a handicrafts center—begun next to his church in 1995 with the help of a St. Mark's teenage group—with our strong backs and our hard dollars.

The concept of a handicraft center is intensely practical. It would train local people, many of them unskilled and unemployed, to produce salable products on the north coast where tourism is important to the economy. When we arrived, the future center was a single cement-block room with a tin roof, and the foundations of a second room. We had sent $500 in advance to help pay for more blocks and cement. Father Carcel wanted us to help erect the walls of the second room and to leave enough additional money for the windows and tin roof. He had hired Ivan Menendez, a local mason, and two helpers for the skill work of mixing the concrete and laying the cement blocks. We would be their helpers. We had come to Honduras expecting to sweat; we would not be disappointed.

Fortified by one of Rosa's substantial breakfasts—orange juice, scrambled eggs, fried beans, tortillas, mangos, pineapple slices, and coffee—we arrived at the work site at 7:30 a.m. Monday to find Ivan and his helpers hard at work. The temperature was already in the mideighties, and the humidity was about 90 percent. Thirty-pound cement blocks from an earlier project were scattered around the site. Our first assignment was to move and stack the blocks near the rising walls of the handicraft center. They seemed heavy at first, but they became lighter after several neighborhood kids about ten years old started picking up blocks to help us. We finished that job about 10:30 a.m. as the temperature soared to 105.

Our second job was more formidable. Using shovels and wheelbarrows, we moved several tons of sand, gravel, and rock from a place in the blazing sun, up an improvised plank ramp, to the construction site; there we dumped our loads, which would later support the floor of the room under construction. We took turns shoveling sand and rocks and muscling the wheelbarrows up the ramp—the men and women doing the same jobs. Father Carcel's charming and deceptively strong wife joined our work crew from time to time, wielding a shovel with panache. Half of us worked for ten or fifteen minutes while the others rested—as time went on, collapsed—in the shade. Liters of drinking water were converted into sweat. By early afternoon, we were exhausted and went for a swim. Ivan and his helpers continued working until sundown each day until the walls were finished. When our group left the following Saturday for the sightseeing part of the trip, we gave Father Carcel a check for $300, which we hoped would be enough for the roof and the windows.

The St. Mark's relationship with the San Marcos cluster is more than blocks and mortar. Over the years we've developed productive and rewarding contacts with people in the villages who are devoted to improving life there—the priests, the teachers, the village elders. We've also talked, language barriers permitting, with ordinary people in all walks of life—people like Ivan the mason, Rosa the cook, waiters and maids, supermarket clerks, Texaco station attendants, and many children. When we were working on the artisan center, a gaggle of neighborhood kids came every day to watch the gringos work. When we finished our work, we all joined in an impromptu and spirited game of "volleyball," played with green balloons I had brought from a Woolworth in Washington.

Music can create important connections. Nadine Hathaway, assisted by interpreter Sondra Berger, spent a morning at the Muchilena elementary school teaching music and percussion instruments. Nadine paid special attention to each child as they sang and laughed together. The school also received a new soccer ball. One evening we gave a community dinner for some fifty people from Muchilena and San Marcos. The cross-lingual conversations were halting, but all the food got eaten.

Two years earlier, Mirian Corea, a bright and talented girl of thirteen, had come to the attention of a St. Mark's group in Muchilena. Mirian is a promising candidate for further education, but her family can't afford to send her to the *colegio* (high school) in nearby Omoa, which, for all expenses, would cost about $400 per year. In Honduras, free public education stops at the sixth grade. Only kids from relatively affluent families attend a *colegio*. The St. Mark's group promised Mirian a scholarship. We sent money to cover the first year's expenses, and Mirian went through seventh grade.

Unfortunately, Mirian's scholarship dropped through the cracks at St. Mark's the following year, and no money was sent for the eighth grade. Such mistakes are not uncommon among church groups that undertake projects for which responsibility is not always clear. In the meantime, Mirian had been farmed out to another family in her village as a live-in maid and baby-sitter in exchange for room and board—a common arrangement among poor Honduran families which can border on indentured servitude.

We found Mirian one morning at her employer's house, broom in hand and surrounded by several small children. Yes, Mirian still wanted to go to high school. We promised her we would follow through this time, spoke with teachers at the school, and made payment arrangements through the bishop's office in San Pedro Sula. I gave Mirian my Spanish-English dictionary.

After a week of work in Muchilena, the group spent the last several days sightseeing. Tela, a north-coast port, featured an exotic rain forest and Punta Sol, an island national park ten miles offshore with monkeys and parrots in the wild. Two of us flew home two days early, skipping the Mayan ruins at Copan.

I've thought a lot about the St. Mark's Honduras project and about outreach in general since my return. It took seven of us two days to move the sand and rock with shovels and wheelbarrows. A bulldozer with a hydraulic shovel could have done the same job in an hour, but that kind of help isn't available gratis to missionary churches on the north coast of Honduras. However, the work we did could have been done in another way—a way which raises questions about who benefits most from some outreach projects, the recipients or the donors.

Each person in our group spent about $1,000 (air fare was $600, the rest was for room, board, transportation, and incidentals) to come to Honduras for ten days—$7,000 for the group. If we had stayed home and instead sent $7,000 to the priests in Omoa and Muchilena, much more—in the way of blocks and mortar—might have been accomplished. Our manual labor at the artisan center could have been done by local laborers, more quickly and for a fraction of the cost. That would have put some money into the pockets of otherwise unemployed Hondurans, instead of American Airlines. Weighed against those benefits, the direct-funding approach would, of course, take from some middle-class gringos the psychic satisfactions of sweating and schmoozing with the less fortunate.

Longtime participants in the Honduras project emphasize its human element—the satisfactions gained from interaction with a person in a faraway land—in a relationship developed over the years, or only in a single conversation. Of course, contacts with people have a warmth and immediacy lacking in long-distance charity, and they can be memorable to those involved. But I question whether they serve the basic purpose of outreach to an impoverished country: to bring about tangible improvements in the daily lives of the people. If poor Honduran *compesinos* were given a choice between money for a water purification facility or occasional conversations with visiting gringos, their choice would be clear.

So why not just stay home and send money? Because it's unlikely that anything approaching the amounts that have been raised and spent at St. Mark's for the Honduras project would have been raised only by appeals for funds—by checkbook charity. There's a world of difference between spending $1,000 for your teenager to go to Honduras for two weeks and being asked to shell out $1,000 for projects and people you'll never see. If I were solicited to support a poor Honduran teenager's high school education,

I might give $5, maybe nothing. But if our Mirian's scholarship were at stake, I might give $100. Experience at St. Mark's shows that the people who go to Honduras, or send their kids there, are the same people who are willing to give generously of their time for fund-raising *and* to write the big checks.

The tangible benefits of outreach might be increased by giving something the recipients don't have and can't get (other than money). One morning in Omoa we encountered a group of nurse practitioners from an Episcopal church in Ocala, Florida, who were on their way to give medical examinations and treatment in remote villages where no medical care was available. Ironically, the same group had just spent a week painting a village church—an activity comparable to our group's moving sand and rocks in wheelbarrows.

The St. Mark's teenagers who go to Honduras undoubtedly receive the greatest benefits from the program and are its strongest justification. Kids can benefit immeasurably from being exposed to another culture and seeing Third World poverty close up. Although direct funding might, theoretically, have done more, the teen projects in Honduras have been valuable to the people there. During an early trip the teens, under adult supervision, built desks and benches for three village schools. Another teen group built a recreation area, including a basketball court and a playground for little kids.

The St. Mark's program would be stronger if teenagers from the Honduran villages could make reciprocal visits to Washington. Unfortunately, the Honduran families don't have the money for that. So far, St. Mark's hasn't had enough for outreach on that scale. Perhaps American Airlines might be persuaded to part with a few free tickets if it got the credit.

It's easy to criticize outreach programs. People who can afford to eat in a restaurant sometimes cadge a free soup-kitchen meal. After my St. Mark's group had spent a "Christmas in April" Saturday sprucing up a ghetto house, two healthy-looking young women in Reeboks returned to the house to inquire whether we were through yet. More generally, it's often true that the givers benefit more than the intended recipients. The St. Mark's Honduras program is one example of that. But that shouldn't matter if such programs are to exist at all.

Some people point to the shortcomings of outreach as excuses not to participate. Despite their shortcomings, outreach programs at St. Mark's and elsewhere undeniably benefit a lot of needy people and deserve to be supported.

Chapter 17

Divorce

Episcopalians think divorce is a sin but you can have as many divorces as you want. It's a paradox.
                    —James Adams, rector, St. Mark's Church

 B y the time our two kids had graduated from college, I think my wife and I both realized that out marriage was dying, again, but neither of us was saying much about it. We were friendly but not close. We didn't laugh as much as we used to, and there were a lot of arguments over trivial things. Despite the warning signals, separation or divorce hadn't crossed my mind. We had been married for twenty-five years, raised two kids, and buried the dog. I expected my wife to bury me, too, when the time came. I was, as the therapists say, in denial.

Things began to come apart in the summer of 1991—symbolized, in my mind, by my wife's three-week trip to Europe to attend a professional conference and visit relatives. When I came home from work to drive her to Dulles Airport for her flight to Copenhagen, she was running late and hadn't finished packing. We dumped her bags in my trunk and discovered, a mile down the road, that her suitcase carrier, a collapsible contraption with wheels, had been left on the kitchen table—a critical oversight my wife blamed on me. I was concentrating on shifting the blame back where I thought it belonged when I missed the beltway turn to the airport, costing us ten precious minutes. We drove on to Dulles, where I spent thirty-five dollars on another suitcase carrier. My wife made her flight with a few minutes to spare, but we were scarcely speaking when she walked down the ramp—an awful way to say good-bye and a harbinger of things to come. We didn't communicate during her absence.

I met my wife at the airport three weeks later. From the time she got off the plane, she was distant. Perhaps I was, too. About a week after her return, we went to a Thai restaurant in Bethesda. There was almost no conversation over dinner. Afterward, she said she needed to talk, and we drove to a park near our home. My wife said she wanted a separation. She pointed out that we had been working on our marriage—including therapy—for years, and that we hadn't been able to maintain a good marriage over time. She didn't want to work on the relationship anymore. I shouldn't have been surprised, but I was. I didn't know what to say.

I was in shock for the next couple of months. I needed a pill or alcohol, usually both, to sleep. We had planned a family vacation on the Outer Banks of North Carolina—where we had been going for years—during the last week of August with our two kids and their friends. My wife opted to stay home, so I went with the kids. I remember walking on the beach with my daughter and trying to explain what had happened, but she wasn't ready to listen and I didn't really know myself. I should have realized that walking the beach would only make my obsessional thinking worse—that I would be better off at work. We left for home a day early.

My wife and I agreed to see a psychiatrist who specializes in marriage counseling. We both liked him—an avuncular figure who looked like Burl Ives. But it soon became apparent that we had different agendas: I wanted to work on the relationship, while my wife was looking for confirmation of her decision. We terminated after a couple of months, with the therapist's concurrence.

I knew I needed more help, so I went back into therapy with a psychiatric social worker I had seen, with good results, for several years in the mid-1980s. I stayed in therapy for about a year, talking almost exclusively about the separation—particularly my part in bringing it about. My marriage was beyond redemption, but I wanted to avoid making the same mistakes later with someone else.

Living under the same roof during this time was intolerable. Fortunately, I had a short-term legal job, which took me to the West Coast about half the time. When I was home, we slept in separate bedrooms. We divided the furniture, the books and records, the kitchen utensils and silverware. I would later regret letting my wife have the old-fashioned icebox I had found in an Iowa barn and later refinished. When we shared a meal, we tried to avoid talking about the marriage—as one can try not to talk about the dead cat on the kitchen table—but the tension remained palpable.

As long as the separation question was in some doubt, we had kept our difficulties to ourselves and a few close friends. I knew my wife had passed the point of no return when she informed me that she was going to tell Rector Jim Adams about our breakup. They had a collegial relationship, having recently taught a fourteen-week confirmation class together. In any case, in a close community like St. Mark's, it seemed appropriate to inform the rector in advance of an event that would cause perturbations in the community. She wrote Jim a note.

I had developed a relationship with Jim Adams during my two years as editor of the *Gospel* and my three years as a member of the Vestry. I called his office for an appointment. I confirmed the coming separation and told Jim something of the circumstances, trying to be objective. We talked for perhaps half an hour. Jim didn't lay any blame or try to change the result. Mostly, he listened. Still, it was a painful meeting.

My wife found an apartment on Connecticut Avenue in the District in mid-November. She brought in her movers a few days before Thanksgiving. When I came home from work that evening, it was a shock to find the living room half empty. I immediately called on a neighbor to help me move our old, wine-stained sofa in from the garage. A few days later, I helped my wife move her plants to her new place. Positioning her plants to catch the morning sun seemed to me to symbolize the end of our twenty-five-year marriage.

Our separation was now a reality and quickly became public information at St. Mark's. Nor were the Kelleys alone. Two other couples, the Osbornes and the Rileys, split up at about the same time. All of us were longtime, active members of the church. Woody Osborne had recently completed two terms as senior warden, the highest elective office in the church. The stuff of delicious gossip, but what else would these developments portend for the congregation, and for me?

Approximately half the marriages in the United States end in divorce. St. Mark's reflects the larger society in that respect—roughly half its adult members have been divorced, a significant number of them more than once. Our associate rector, Susan Gresinger, was divorced long before she came to St. Mark's. One of Jim Adams's daughters, herself an Episcopal priest, recently divorced. To adapt a Karl Menninger statement about violence: "Divorce is as American as apple pie." One might think that a sophisticated, caring community like St. Mark's would accept a coreligionist's decision to end a marriage and support him (or her) in a time of severe distress.

The first few Sundays after I talked to Jim Adams, I sat alone toward the back of the church. I was sure everyone knew my wife and I had separated, but none of my friends said anything to me about it during coffee.

If I raised the subject, the typical response was silence or a change of topic. One Sunday morning, I ran into Scilla Adams in the hallway. She had been one of the teachers in my confirmation class. We stopped, facing each other. There was an awkward pause, then Scilla said, "I don't know what to say." I started to cry, and she joined me. Then I said, "It doesn't matter what you say, Scilla. At least you said something."

St. Mark's was the only community my wife and I had shared. There was no community life around our home in Chevy Chase, and our work had few social dimensions. About three-quarters of our social life—dinner parties, dances, weekends away—had grown out of the church. My social life died—almost completely—along with my marriage, at a time when I needed personal contacts more than ever before. My church friends disappeared into the stained glass.

At first I was puzzled by the silent treatment at St. Mark's and the silence of my phone at home. These people had been my friends for years. These were sophisticated city dwellers accustomed to divorces and other nonconformities. Why were they finding it so difficult to talk about the central reality of my life? Why didn't they invite me to the party?

My friend Bill Repsher contended that couples gravitate socially toward other couples—that's their "comfort zone"—and when you cease to be a couple, you're out. That sounded to me like an oversimplification for what was really going on. I became convinced that many married couples are profoundly upset by the divorce of another couple in their circle—there but for the grace of God go we. Here we are, playing by the rules, struggling along in our own imperfect union, when another couple decides to break the rules. The prospect of divorce and the devastating losses and disruptions it would entail are simply too painful to contemplate. Paradoxically, there's probably some jealousy and anger mixed with the fear. Why do others get to start over when we're stuck in an often unrewarding union?

There were other less plausible explanations for my feelings of isolation. I thought I might have been riding my wife's social coattails, with her more likable personality offsetting my abrasiveness, until now. It's often said that friends of a couple choose sides in a divorce. In our separation, however, close mutual friends stuck with both of us. Casual friends and acquaintances either remained friendly or dropped both of us.

Overall, I was disappointed in my church community's response to my separation. But there were exceptions. Rich and Kathryn Chafetz, both of whom have been divorced, invited me over one evening before Christmas.

They introduced me to a friend of theirs who happened to drop by—an attractive blonde and the estranged wife of a member of Rich's book club. Rich later invited me to join his book club, which proved an enjoyable social outlet until the blonde's husband got upset about my dating his wife.

Hayden Boyd, my motorcycle buddy, and his wife, Margot, invited me and my kids to Christmas dinner. And Hayden invited me to join his book club after I had to drop out of Rich's book club. Ann Craig went to dinner with me when her husband, Roger, was teaching a Christian education class with my wife.

Separation and divorce can raise a sticky issue for a couple at St. Mark's: who stays, who goes, or do both stay? Jim Adams reports that church membership has sometimes been treated as property in divorces, with the settlement agreement specifying which party has to leave. It may work well enough for both parties to stay if, for example, both become happily remarried; but it takes time for that to occur, if it ever does. In most of the divorces I've seen at St. Mark's, one former spouse has found another church. I doubt whether I would ever have been comfortable with both my former wife and I staying active in the same church. After our separation, I became more heavily involved at St. Mark's. She became less active and later joined another church.

Although I was an outcast from the St. Mark's social circuit, the church was a resource in other ways. I was a member of a small men's group that met monthly to talk about our victories and defeats over beer and pretzels. During those first months after the separation, I took most of the airtime. The other three members of the group had all been divorced. They made good listeners.

That fall the men's class was being offered—eight weeks plus a weekend in Rehoboth, Delaware. There were interesting names on the sign-up sheet, but, under the circumstances, I would have signed up with almost anyone. I liked being around Peter Byrne, a professor at Georgetown Law who appreciates my sense of humor; Rob Hall, a lobbyist and former football player; and David Evelyn, a high school art teacher. Equally important, the class got me out of the house once a week during the grimmest fall of my life.

This book was in the germinal stages at that time. It had occurred to me, however, that if I were to pursue the idea I might not remember enough about my early years at St. Mark's, particularly about the introduction and confirmation classes. Jim Adams granted my request to help him teach the introduction class, which he usually taught alone. I brought a skeptical voice to a class of twenty-five bright and eager young people, many of whom seemed quite skeptical themselves. That I got out of the house one night a week in the dark of winter was a bonus.

Among its other functions, St. Mark's is a dating bureau. Many a divorced member has found new love at a Sunday service or in a Christian education class. By the time spring arrived, I had recovered from the initial shock and was beginning to put a new life together. I considered dating women at St. Mark's, but I didn't want to fuel any more gossip than I already had. I was also leery of dating someone, stopping, and then sitting next to her in a service.

One weekend that first summer as a single, I went with Hayden Boyd on an aimless motorcycle ride in southern Pennsylvania, ending up in Altoona. On the way, we passed through the hamlet of Carnes, which happened to be the last name of my girlfriend in law school. She had left me for another and broken my heart. Later she had divorced her first husband and, the last I knew, had gone to Australia with number two. Sitting on my motorcycle in a parking lot in Altoona, I decided to call her mother in Iowa for current information. Mrs. Carnes, then in her eighties, received my call cordially and told me that her daughter was divorced and living in Boulder, Colorado; she asked if I would like to have the phone number. Delightful reunions in Boulder and Washington, D.C., followed. I soon concluded, however, that commuting relationships of a thousand miles or more are not practical. So I switched my attention to the personal ads in Washington, with mixed results. But that's another story.

After about a year as a social pariah at St. Mark's, I became disillusioned to the point of shopping for another church. One Sunday I went to St. Albans next to the National Cathedral, where I heard a sermon by Jack Danforth, the senator from Missouri and an Episcopal priest. I liked the sermon but didn't like the little communion wafers (instead of bread). I didn't like the fact that the priest read all the announcements, and besides, the congregation looked old and stuffy. Another Sunday I went to St. Columba's, a thriving, if rather staid, church in an affluent section of northwest Washington. The sermon by the charismatic former rector of Trinity Church, Copley Square in Boston was brilliant and moving, but, again, I felt no affinity with the congregation. I still felt some resentment toward St. Mark's, but it was looking better and better by comparison.

One Sunday morning more than a year after the separation, Janice

Gregory delivered the senior warden's annual state-of-the-church sermon. She caught my attention when she said: "Our practice of caring for each other in a concrete way when we face personal crisis was tested again and again this past year—by divorce, separation, illness, unemployment, family crises, and death. And each time our community response has been, to the best of our ability, open and direct, without trying to hide the pain."

During the comment period after her sermon, I stood up to take exception, saying that, prior to my separation:

> I had come to rely very heavily on St. Mark's for support. A large part of my social life and many of my friendships are down here. I wouldn't analogize it to shunning in a Quaker meeting, but I will tell you that a great many people in this church whom I had considered friends and from whom I thought I could expect something have avoided me like the plague. If I were going to grade St. Mark's on giving a caring response to separated people, I'd say maybe a C minus. Last summer I gave serious thought to leaving this church for that reason. I looked around and finally decided that St.Mark's probably isn't any *worse* than other churches when it comes to divorce. Since there are other things to be said in its favor, I decided to stick around.

I was touched when Quin Hillyer, a member of the intro class I had helped Jim Adams teach a year earlier, got up after me and said:

> I don't know how St. Mark's has responded to you in your difficulty, but [when you taught the intro class] you responded by giving to St. Mark's. And your giving helped me get into this wonderful place, which has kept me afloat for the last year. One thing you might look at: Did St. Mark's have something to do with your ability to give in the midst of your crisis? Because give you did, and I thank you for it.

When a couple decides to marry, the proposed union is announced from the pulpit and the congregation is told, "If any of you know just cause why they may not be joined together in Holy Matrimony, you are bidden to declare it." Nobody ever objects, but the banns are a quaint custom. The happy couple usually stands up as people clap and cheer.

Joe Tarantolo is a psychiatrist who takes a dim view of divorce. Concerned about the prevalence of divorce at St. Mark's, Joe wrote a *Gospel* piece in which he called for a "Banns of Divorce" ritual modeled on the traditional "Banns of Marriage." Joe's idea was that a proposed separation or divorce should be announced from the pulpit like a marriage so that parishioners would have an opportunity to voice any objections. His thesis was that the congregation is injured by a failure to honor marriage vows and that therefore it has a legitimate interest in whether the divorce should take place. Implicit in his proposal was that a Banns of Divorce ritual would actually prevent some separations and divorces from happening.

Joe's proposal made me angry. I think decisions to separate or divorce are private matters, subjects one discusses only with close friends or possibly a therapist or priest. It seems absurd to suggest that negative comments from a church congregation could affect such decisions. In short, I thought this was none of the congregation's business. I submitted a responding piece to the *Gospel* making those points.

Nothing came of the Banns of Divorce proposal, but the *Gospel* articles and a few more divorces—including a highly visible young couple active in the Christian education program—caused a lot of murmuring among the married couples who were hanging in there. Associate Rector Susan Gresinger weighed in with her *Gospel* article on separation and divorce. I agreed with most of what she had to say, except for her view that divorce is sinful and those who break their marriage vows should seek forgiveness.

I did my share to destroy my marriage—perhaps more than my share—but for a long time I struggled against the notion that I had sinned. I wasn't some flake—married and divorced three times in five years. I had stayed married for twenty-five years; helped raise my two children into responsible adults; been faithful to my wife; and spent years in couples therapy "working on the relationship," as the saying goes.

I later talked to Susan Gresinger about the theological and psychological implications of divorce. She agreed that, for some, divorce may be the best of several bad choices. Some people, realistically, can't keep their marital vows—an extreme example, victims of physical abuse. Even so, as Susan saw it: "The road back to health isn't celebration of a new start. Instead, it involves acknowledging that I couldn't, wouldn't, do what I said I would do, and for that I feel sorry. Forgiveness means that the behavior is put behind me and I'm free to move on with my life. I don't see that—becoming reconciled to what happened—as a bad way to respond to divorce."

Neither do I.

Chapter 18

Aging and Dying

Shall I part my hair behind? Do I dare to eat a peach?
I shall wear white flannel trousers, and walk upon the beach.
　　　—T. S. Eliot, "The Love Song of J. Alfred Prufrock"

The riders in a race do not stop short when they reach the goal.
There is always a little finishing canter.
　　　　　　　—Oliver Wendell Holmes, Jr.,
　　　　　　　　radio address on his ninetieth birthday

When I was twenty-five, like most people I thought I was immortal. I still felt that way at forty. I could stay up late, drink a lot, and work hard the next day. Or take a nasty spill on a ski slope and go right back up the lift for another run. I almost never saw a doctor. Nobody I knew died, except in accidents that wouldn't happen to me.

As I finish this book, I'm sixty-one—not old by today's standards. I have all my hair. After my last physical exam, the doctor pronounced my health "generally good"; his suggestions were modest: lose ten pounds and lower my cholesterol level twenty points. That sounded reassuring, yet when I get out of bed in the morning—slowly now—my back, my neck, one hip or the other hurts; sometimes two or three parts hurt at the same time. My sight and hearing aren't what they used to be, several molars are crowned, my interest in sex is diminished, and I'm usually in bed by eleven. I know the machine is wearing out. Eventually it will cease to function.

It wasn't a coincidence that I began coming to St. Mark's at forty-seven—after my father died and I began to ache getting up in the morning. And it wasn't that I wanted to hedge my bet by acknowledging a God who would punish me if I persisted in unbelief. After fifteen years at St. Mark's, I still expect to die a skeptic who believes death brings oblivion. Still, I've found that a church like St. Mark's has a lot to offer skeptical people who are aging, burying their parents, and starting to face the inevitability of their own deaths.

Aging is harder when you're living alone, as I have lived for the five years since my separation and divorce. I'm fortunate to be growing older connected to people about my age at St. Mark's—several close friends and a number of other people I know well enough to care about, and to attend their funerals if they die ahead of me. Whenever getting old is getting to me, it's comforting to see the thinning hair, crow's-feet, and turkey wattles around me on Sunday morning.

Role models, religious and other (from Jesus Christ to Michael Jordan), have always been with us. Although they haven't been designated as such, St. Mark's has role models for the aging—people who are living out their late years productively, with humor and dignity. The Craighills are a good example.

One Sunday morning not long after I discovered St. Mark's, the service included a liturgical dance. One of the dancers was a tall, slender, graying man in a black leotard who appeared to be about seventy. Although it has an ancient and honored place in church history, I'm not usually enthusiastic about liturgical dance. My literal-mindedness makes it hard for me to understand, and, most of the time, I experience dance as an interruption of the service, not a contribution. That morning, however, I was taken by the old man dancing—by his athleticism and grace—and I admired his courage to dance for an audience in a leotard.

Bowdoin ("Bowdie") Craighill, eighty-two, is the warden emeritus of St. Mark's. Bowdie was born in Washington and has lived and practiced law here most of his life. While in law school, he dated Mary Jackson (daughter of Attorney General Robert Jackson, later a justice of the U.S. Supreme Court), whom he later married. Anticipating World War II, Bowdie enlisted in the navy in 1940 as an apprentice seaman. He became a "ninety-day wonder," was commissioned as an officer, and then assigned to the anti-aircraft cruiser USS *Atlanta*. In 1942, the American and Japanese fleets fought off Guadalcanal, and the *Atlanta* was hit by heavy shellfire and two Japanese torpedoes. Bowdie received the Silver Star for his firefighting that night. The *Atlanta* was scuttled the next day.

Bowdie Craighill has been an active member of St. Mark's for thirty-six years. He was first elected to the Vestry in 1963. As senior warden in 1966, Bowdie was a member of the committee that recommended Jim Adams as the new rector. After that, he was chancellor (legal adviser) to the bishop of Washington for five years.

Most of Bowdie's service to the church was before my time, but I've valued our contacts since coming to St. Mark's. I attended a "Parish Managers' Weekend" with Bowdie and about twenty others at Claggett, a depressing former orphanage in the country north of Washington which St. Mark's uses for conferences when no better site is available. Whatever its shortcomings, Claggett does have an outdoor basketball court. On Saturday afternoon, I came upon Bowdie shooting hoops—free throws, soft hook shots in the low post, and sedate jump shots from the top of the key. I challenged him to a game of "horse," which he won. Bowdie neglected to mention that he had played Southeast Conference basketball at the University of the South in 1935, the year I was born.

Mary Craighill, Bowdie's wife of forty-four years, first became involved in liturgical dance in the 1950s in a McLean, Virginia, church. Looking for an opportunity to move into the District, she went to lunch at "the Monocle" on Capitol Hill with then Rector Bill Baxter and Senior Warden Harry McPherson, a senior aide to President Lyndon Johnson. The ostensible purpose of the lunch was to discuss moving Mary's dance company to St. Mark's. Baxter and McPherson talked politics through lunch; nothing was said about the dance company. When Mary finally pressed Bill about the terms for moving her company, he said, "You get the studio, and we get the dance company's services whenever we want." That's been the understanding ever since.

Bill Baxter could not have envisioned the St. Mark's Dance Studio of the 1990s—a bustling place of three hundred students whose standouts have toured the former Soviet Union and the Czech Republic in recent years. At seventy-five, Mary Craighill continues as director of the Studio, which offers ballet, modern dance, jazz, and exercise. Mary is teaching and choreographing full-time, using a cane after a spine fusion operation to correct a dance injury. She was pictured in a recent *Time* magazine article about aging that featured her classmate at Smith College, Betty Friedan.

My mother, ninety-four, has lived for the past eight years in an Episcopal retirement community just outside the Washington, D.C., beltway. She had a full life there—concerts at the Kennedy Center, plays at Arena Stage, drinks before dinner, bridge four times a week, Trivial Pursuit on Friday night—until she fell, broke her hip, and hip replacement surgery failed.

After her fall, my mother had to give up her apartment—furnished from home with her mother's antiques—for round-the-clock care. When she was transferred to the nursing floor after surgery, she was in severe pain and, as she told me repeatedly, wanted only to die. I've always known my mother as a proud and articulate woman. She taught high school English for many years and, without much urging, would recite the dagger scene from *Macbeth* or the prologue to the *Canterbury Tales*. Two years of helplessness in her bed or wheelchair—without her bridge partners, her trips to town, and her bourbon highballs—have dimmed her agile mind and dampened her spirit. She still knows who I am and sometimes seems to know where she is. But she slips in and out of delusional states, doesn't read or even watch *Jeopardy,* her favorite television show, and she sleeps most of the time. I visit my mother once or twice a week as I wait for her to die.

"Me and My Aging Parents," a Christian education course at St. Mark's, helped prepare me for my mother's lingering death. I had taken the course years before my mother broke her hip. I was trying, at fifty, to learn how to act like an adult when confronted with her strong, sometimes controlling personality. Several in the class had mothers like mine had been in her prime; we found it easier to see the other person's regressions and failures than our own, but we came away with a clearer appreciation of our own.

The class focused on the elderly, disabled parent. How much do I owe my mother (or father) when she can no longer live independently? Do I let her move in with my active family? What if there isn't enough money for a good nursing home and for my kids' college education? Some questions had a harsh, selfish ring. Should I look for a less expensive care option so there is something left to inherit? Do I still have to visit Mother after she no longer knows who I am? When that happens, what should be done to keep her alive? Should medication be terminated to speed her death? I tended toward selfish answers to these questions, while others seemed prepared to sacrifice more for their parents, and to keep them alive when the parent no longer had any real quality of life. Of course, there are no "right" answers to such questions, only your answers. But it helps to talk with others before your time comes to face them.

St. Mark's isn't a morbid place, quite the contrary. We laugh a lot, dance in the church, and throw banana cream pies at the rector during fund-raisers. But we try to maintain a healthy awareness of death as a part of life—through symbols, sermons, classes—and, of course, funerals.

The Tiffany stained-glass window depicting Jesus' last walk through the streets of Jerusalem dominates our worship space from the north wall. A stark wooden cross is suspended over the altar in the center of the nave.

At the far end of the church is a columbarium—a series of niches recessed in the wall to hold the ashes of the dead. Most of the vaults bear names indicating they've been reserved; those that also bear dates are occupied.

Death can make a provocative sermon topic. Jim Adams preached a Lenten sermon about three common attitudes toward death, which he called the heroic, the romantic, and the practical. The heroic is what the name implies: laying down your life for a cause—noble, yes; suicidal, perhaps; but in any case, not for most of us. The dying romantic plans his own funeral to the last detail: the hymns, the flowers, the eulogies—an exquisite and moving event. It's a pity the romantic can't be there to enjoy it.

The Woody Allen movie *Hannah and Her Sisters* reminded Adams of how one can approach death as a purely practical matter, just another in the train of biological events in life. In the movie, the Allen character bewails his imminent death from brain cancer. His father, the practical one, points out that his son hadn't worried about being alive before he was born, so why should he be upset about not being alive after he's dead? In his sermon Adams suggested a healthier attitude toward death, derived from St. Paul. Paul gives us permission to hate the thought of dying, to say, "The fear of death troubles me." And to say freely and openly, "That's the way it is."

Death is an important theme in the introduction and confirmation classes (chapter 4) taken by nearly all members. Functional education classes about death have been offered since Jim Adams wrote his first book, *The Sting of Death,* in 1971. Next year, I'll be one of the teachers in a functional class about death.

Ernest Becker's *The Denial of Death* won the Pulitzer Prize for nonfiction in 1974. The *New York Times Book Review* called the book "a brave work of electrifying intelligence and passion, optimistic and revolutionary, destined to endure." Becker, a professor of cultural anthropology at the University of California at Berkeley (and something of a cult hero there during the restless 1970s), was dying of cancer when he wrote the book.

Sheila Turpin-Foster invited me to join her in leading a series of group discussions of *The Denial of Death* one summer at St. Mark's. The book makes for difficult reading. Chapter eight, for example, "Otto Rank and the Closure of Psychoanalysis on Kierkegaard," escaped me almost entirely. Still, I benefited more from one central idea in *The Denial of Death* than from anything I had read for many years—perhaps since reading Albert Camus's *The Plague* as an undergraduate.

Becker recalls Samuel Johnson's observation: "The prospect of death wonderfully concentrates the mind." Building on Johnson, Becker states: "The fear of death haunts the human animal like nothing else; it is a mainspring of human activity, designed to avoid the finality of death, to overcome it by denying it as the final destiny of man." How can death be denied? For Becker, "our central calling, our main task on this planet" is to deny death metaphorically, to be "a hero, to make the biggest possible contribution to world life, to show that [I] *count* more then anything or anyone else." (Emphasis in the original.)

Becker sees life as a "fascinating opportunity to expand . . . [to] realize my distinctive gifts, make my own contribution to the world through my own self-expansion." For those who choose the heroic path, who try to "realize their distinctive gifts," their work is "at the same time the expression of [their] heroism and the justification of it. . . . Its uniqueness gives [them] personal immortality."

Why don't we all become heroes? In modern culture "the heroic seems too big for us, or we too small for it. Tell a young man that he is entitled to be hero and he will blush." Becker goes on to suggest that most of us avoid growth, set low levels of aspiration, and engage in "self-crippling pseudo-stupidity" as "defenses against grandiosity"—that is, defenses against being a hero. There are, of course, some good practical reasons for such avoidance and denial. Those who choose the heroic path separate themselves from the herd. They become isolated and "exposed to the sense of being completely crushed."

When I read *The Denial of Death* in 1989 I had recently opened a solo law office in Rockville, Maryland. I liked being on my own after twenty years on a government payroll, but I came to dislike handling divorces, trying fender-bender lawsuits, and defending drunk drivers—grist in the mill for a solo practitioner trying to get started. Partly because of my somewhat disdainful attitude, I wasn't very good at the work, either. As I waited in court for my client's case to be called (trial lawyers do an inordinate amount of waiting), I would reflect on how unhappy I was. Surely, I thought, I'm on Earth for some better purpose. But I wasn't acting on those reflections. Becker probably would have called my pedestrian law practice my "defense against grandiosity."

I've always been a good writer. When the law business was slow, I started dabbling in freelance writing, sold a couple of articles to magazines, and began to think about writing for a living. *The Denial of Death* gave me a strong shove in that direction—as Becker would say, to "realize my distinctive gifts, make my own contribution to the world." In 1992, three years after reading Becker's book, I closed my law office for good. I've been writing full-time since then; this is my second book. After four years without any significant income from writing, I expect to make some money from sales of my first book next year.

Of course, I won't really cheat death with my writing. But if I write well, my books will be around for a while after I'm not. I don't feel particularly heroic (Becker's word) about giving up a secure but spirit-killing law practice for the largely psychic rewards of writing. But the knowledge that I'm creating something uniquely mine and, I hope, of some value to others gives me a sense that my life is worthwhile. I complain about the isolation of writing, but I can tolerate that in exchange for the freedom, in my sixties, to say and do pretty much as I please—a freedom others have valued:

> "You are old Father William," the young man said,
>   "And your hair has become very white;
> And yet you incessantly stand on your head—
>   Do you think, at your age, it is right?"
> —Lewis Carroll, *Alice's Adventures in Wonderland*

Afterword:
Finding an Open Church

When you're in a place where you feel safe, where you feel you can explore and question things, it's you discovering on your own what it means. It's not somebody telling you what it means.
—Jennie Bevington, member, All Saints Episcopal Church,
Pasadena, California, quoted in
MacNeil/Lehrer NewsHour, July 18, 1995

Jennie Bevington and her husband, Eric, are baby boomers, two of the 76 million Americans born in the twenty years following World War II and now ranging in age from thirty to fifty. Boomers like Bill Clinton are assuming leadership roles in politics, in business, in academe, and throughout American society. Almost all baby boomers received some sort of religious upbringing, but two-thirds later dropped out. Forty percent of the dropouts, however, have since returned to church. Representing one-third of the population, the boomers (plus their children) are the major consumers of organized religion in the United States today. It is their spiritual needs that churches now competing for members are challenged to meet.

In July 1995, Richard Ostling, *Time* magazine's religion writer and a contributing correspondent to the *MacNeil/Lehrer NewsHour,* looked at the impact of the baby-boomer generation on organized religion, focusing on two churches representing very different positions on questions of faith: Saddleback Valley Community Church in Orange County, California, a conservative evangelical church affiliated with the Southern Baptists; and All Saints Episcopal Church in Pasadena, California, a liberal, mainline church similar to St. Mark's in its questioning orientation. Ostling spoke with the ministers of both churches, bringing out similarities as well as differences between conservative Saddleback and liberal All Saints.

Both churches have large and active congregations, most of whom are of baby boomers. Sermons speak directly to parishioners' day-to-day concerns—about drugs, divorce, abortion—not to theological abstractions. Hymn and choir singing are integral to services. Activities at both Saddleback and All Saints extend beyond Sunday services to support groups of all kinds, to twelve-step recovery programs, and to outreach activities linking the church to the community. But when it comes to matters of belief, the similarities end.

According to *Time*'s Ostling: "In the liberal churches [like All Saints], faith is an open-ended exploration. But in the evangelical congregations [like Saddleback], faith is based on a strict and conservative view of Bible teaching." The ministers of the two churches agreed with Ostling's description of their basic difference. Rick Warren, the minister of Saddleback, saw his job this way:

> Baby boomers are looking for some kind of solution in answer to life. In the 60s they tried rebellion and drugs. In the 70s they tried sex and therapy, and in the 80s they tried making money. And now they're going through middle age and they're saying, what's next, what's left? We give people a purpose to live for that gives them significance and meaning. They get up in the morning and say this is what I'm living for, and it makes all the difference in the world.

George Regas, rector of All Saints, was wary of giving parishioners too many answers:

> The conservative evangelical church [like Saddleback] gives a sense of security. Life is very tumultuous, very uncertain, and there's something attractive about those certitudes. But there is something unwise about the presentation of the Gospel that says: we will give you certitude. The Christian faith is an adventure and God's grace is with us as we make our way in this journey into God, and there is no certainty there.

In this book, I hope to say something helpful to skeptics, thoughtful people who received a religious upbringing—Protestant, Catholic, or Jewish—but who later rejected their faiths as a matter of considered intellectual conviction. The *MacNeil/Lehrer* sketch of the dichotomy between conservative evangelical churches like Saddleback, where people go for answers, and liberal churches like All Saints, where people go to ask questions, provides a useful perspective from which an unchurched skeptic can begin to look at churches in the United States today.

Conservative churches, in addition to the evangelicals, include fundamentalists, charismatics, and pentecostals, which differ among themselves but are alike in giving their members definite answers. Here are some typical answers one would be given in a conservative church with a strong fundamentalist orientation: God created the world in six days (Darwin was wrong), He rescued Jonah from the belly of the whale, Jesus walked on the water, and so on through a long list of incredible events in the Bible. And in virtually all conservative churches, the minister has the answers to questions of faith, answers which parishioners are expected to accept.

Until recently, growth trends of the conservative churches at the national level had been upward, but those trends have begun to flatten out. Memberships in the mainline Protestant churches, including the Episcopal Church, have been declining for years, but those rates of decline are lessening. There are indications that the only real growth is among the unchurched—the people to whom this book is mainly addressed.

Skeptics who left conservative churches—Roman Catholic, Southern Baptist, Assembly of God—when they were young tend to associate all churches with unquestioning acceptance of unbelievable things and conclude, understandably, that churches have nothing to offer them. Many are concerned, as I was, that joining a church that prays to a God they don't believe in would compromise their intellectual integrity and fill their children's heads with superstitious nonsense. Beyond that, their early religious experiences may have been painful, even psychologically damaging, as was my experience in the Catholic Church. So they stay away from churches, except for weddings and funerals.

I've tried to show through my experience at St. Mark's how a church can welcome skeptics and enrich their lives without forcing them to sacrifice their intellectual integrity—how a church can be a place to raise questions, not just listen to the minister's answers. At St. Mark's, we read from the Bible and recite the Nicene Creed because they're important sources of the Christian tradition and, sometimes, evocative metaphors for our lives, but no one is expected to take them literally, and few do. Far from passive acceptance of dogma, questions are encouraged, and there is room for healthy irreverence. It's become a standing joke that St. Mark's Christian education program teaches people to say the Nicene Creed with a straight face. But freedom of belief—including the freedom not to believe—is only part of what attracted me back to church. Diversity in membership, shared authority between the clergy and members, and a vibrant community life are important, too.

Many mainline Protestant congregations have a typical profile: old, white, wealthy, doctrinaire, sexist, and autocratic, not to mention a buttoned-down dress code. These former bastions of the faith are the ones that are shrinking fastest, losing members to death and the indifference of those who find them irrelevant. But some liberal Protestant churches, most of them in urban areas, are growing by attracting diverse congregations—including young people, blacks and Hispanics, gays and lesbians, agnostics and atheists. Increased vitality in the church community and sensitivity to feminist concerns usually go along with diversity in membership. Diversity and vitality are sometimes accompanied by more democratic ways of running the church. When these elements coalesce, they form a church that might be variously described as liberal, progressive, welcoming, or inclusive. I prefer the word "open" because it implies not only diversity of membership but also open-mindedness in matters of belief and a willingness to consider new ways of operating—the kind of church a skeptic might be interested in.

 Open churches don't exhibit the characteristics of openness to the same degree, as shown by a comparison of St. Mark's with St. Margaret's, another downtown Episcopal church in Washington, D.C. St. Mark's is the most open church in the Washington area when it comes to welcoming skeptical people. But its congregation, while somewhat diverse, is mostly white and middle-class (see chapter 5).

I spoke with Episcopal priest Jim Steen, a member of St. Margaret's and then its acting rector, about skepticism and diversity there. Agnostics find St. Margaret's open, or at least not rejecting; some are active members. Unlike at St. Mark's, however, no special efforts are made to attract them, and they tend to blend in with the rest of the congregation. Apart from skeptics, however, diversity (the current church word for it is "inclusiveness")—has been an active commitment at St. Margaret's for a decade. The church is ideally located to meet that commitment, situated at the intersection of Connecticut and Florida Avenues, a few blocks west of the Adams-Morgan area (heavily Hispanic and black), just north of Du Pont Circle (a large gay and lesbian population), and abutting the Kalorama area (white and wealthy). Steen estimates that the congregation at St. Margaret's is 15 to 20 percent black, 10 to 15 percent gay and lesbian, with some Hispanic and Asian members. It includes the very rich and the very poor, the highly educated and some with virtually no education.

Steen recalls a Sunday when a homeless man made his way to a pew near the front, looking very hungry. The rector stopped the service and said: "Charley is hungry. Who is going to see to it that Charley gets something to eat?" The rector didn't continue the service until someone volunteered to take the man out for food.

The "open church" I've described is, of course, a theoretical ideal. There probably is no church that fully meets all my criteria: a questioning approach, welcoming to skeptics; a diverse congregation; an active community life; and shared authority, with opportunities open to all. Whether a particular church qualifies as open can be debatable. There are churches that like to think of themselves as "open" (it sounds more Christian than "closed") but aren't. The Episcopal Church has some "Junior League" parishes run by wealthy, straight white people who like to have minorities— blacks, Hispanics, gays, and lesbians—in the pews on Sunday because it makes them feel good. But they don't want those people running their club from the Vestry or the Worship Committee.

Suppose some of my skeptical readers decide to look at an open church. How are they going to find one where they live? It may be easy in some places, impossible in others. Open churches, while growing in number, are the exception, not the rule. There are no directories identifying churches as open or closed, conservative or liberal, and I was in no position to conduct a survey. In writing this chapter, I relied on my own experience at St. Mark's and in visiting other churches, on selected readings in the sociology of religion, and on interviews with Episcopal priests. Given that background, my conclusions about the prevalence of the open church are necessarily tentative, as are my suggestions for finding one.

I focus on the Episcopal Church because St. Mark's has been my spiritual home and community for the past fifteen years. I don't mean to imply that openness can't be found in other denominations, but my knowledge of them is limited. I understand that of the mainline Protestant churches, the two most liberal—and therefore most likely to be hospitable to openness—are the Episcopal Church and the United Church of Christ (the result of a merger of the former Congregational and other churches). The United Church of Christ may be somewhat more liberal than the Episcopal Church; it's the only mainline church so far to sanction ordination of gays and lesbians. The Presbyterian, Methodist, and Lutheran Churches are relatively conservative.

The Unitarian Universalist Church (also a product of earlier mergers) is an option for skeptics in search of community. Many Unitarians don't describe themselves as Christians and, indeed, don't embrace any particular religious faith, seeking wisdom in different religions. They pay attention to social issues. They value a questioning approach and rational analysis, as skeptics do. But the Unitarians have no liturgy, no ritual, no prayers. A Unitarian friend of mine speaks of "going to the Sunday morning lecture." Skeptics who value liturgy and prayer, even though they don't take the words literally and are interested in spiritual growth, however defined, are unlikely to have their needs met in a Unitarian Universalist Church.

In Washington, D.C., I know of three Episcopal churches that clearly qualify as open: St. Mark's, St. Margaret's, and St. Stephen and the Incarnation. (There may be others.) It's no accident that all three are located in the downtown area. Open churches in the suburbs are extremely rare. Jim Adams, former rector of St. Mark's, thinks that an open church can be found in virtually any major city, citing churches he has visited in Atlanta and Houston as examples. Jim Steen generally agrees with Adams, adding Miami and Dallas as places where he knows of open churches. Both agree, however, that finding one might take some looking, even in a major city.

Open churches scarcely exist in small towns or even in small to medium-sized cities. Small towns—like my hometown of Algona, Iowa—tend to have homogenous populations with conservative religious views. A skeptic looking for an open church in Iowa might be best advised to try Des Moines (the state's largest city) or Iowa City (where the university is located and skepticism is in the air). I spoke recently with a former member of St. Mark's who moved three years ago to Akron, Ohio. She reported that she has been looking for an open church in the Akron area but has been unable to find one.

A liberal bishop can influence the character of churches throughout his diocese. Bishop John Spong of the Diocese of Newark, New Jersey, is the most prominent liberal bishop in the Episcopal Church. He is the author of many books, including *Rescuing the Bible from Fundamentalism* (Harper, 1992) and *Living in Sin: A Bishop Rethinks Human Sexuality* (Harper & Row, 1988). Marked degrees of openness characterize many of the churches in Spong's Diocese of Newark. Notable among them is Church of the Redeemer in Morristown, New Jersey. At Bishop Spong's suggestion, I talked to its rector, the Reverend Philip Wilson, about who comes to Redeemer and what happens there.

Church of the Redeemer ranks high in diversity. Morristown, once home to Rockefellers and Vanderbilts, is still a wealthy community, but it also has poor people and typical urban problems. Redeemer's congregation of about four hundred includes CEOs and street people. Agnostics and atheists come openly and in numbers. Blacks represent 5 to 10 percent of the congregation. About half of Redeemer's members are gay or lesbian, in roughly equal numbers. Over half of the congregation are former Roman Catholics.

Some Redeemer members drive an hour to get there, passing other churches. More than diversity draws them. Redeemer may be unique among Episcopal churches in describing itself, first of all, as a "liberation" church—liberation from whatever it is that keeps people from being themselves. Martin Luther King Day is celebrated as much as Easter. Redeemer rents a bus for the annual gay-pride parade. The liberation concept means different things to different people—blacks, gays, alcoholics, agnostics—but it does draw them together.

Liberation at Redeemer takes precedence over being Christian—God, Philip Wilson notes, isn't a Christian—and over Episcopalian tradition whenever those values come into conflict. The Nicene Creed doesn't meet Redeemer's standards of inclusiveness and isn't included in the Sunday service. In the traditional Episcopal communion, bread and wine are offered and the priest eats and drinks first. At Redeemer, grape juice is an option and the priest, the servant of the people, eats and drinks last—including Bishop Spong when he visits.

One block down South Street from Church of the Redeemer is St. Peter's, another Episcopal church with a congregation about triple Redeemer's size. St. Peter's is the more traditional, with an Anglican-style men and boys' choir and other trappings. Bishop Spong lives in Morristown and is a member of St. Peter's. Philip Wilson recalls Spong saying, "I love Redeemer, but I only want one in my diocese." In 1996, Bishop Spong named Redeemer "Church of the Year."

This suggests that an open church may be relatively easy to find in the Diocese of Newark, which includes much of northern New Jersey. What about the rest of the country? You can't tell from the advertisments in the Saturday paper; they all sound more or less alike. In any case, only a few of the hundreds of churches in a major city—there are 125 Episcopal churches in the Washington, D.C., diocese—buy a newspaper ad. St. Mark's, for example, doesn't.

Word of mouth can be a good source of information. Like-minded people one knows may be members of an open church and invite a newcomer to attend a service with them. Most people come to church for the first time because they've been invited by a friend. But what if one is new in town?

Jim Steen of St. Margaret's suggests that an interested person could call the minister or pastor and say: "I'm looking for a church. What can you tell me about yours?" If that question were put to him, Steen thought he would say something like this: "St. Margaret's prides itself on being inclusive. This is a place where all kinds of people at all kinds of places in their faith journey are very welcome. If that's the kind of place you're looking for, you couldn't do better."

Open churches may become more numerous, and easier to find, in the future. The Center for Progressive Christianity, recently founded by Jim Adams and based in Cambridge, Massachusetts, seeks to promote an understanding of Christianity that places more emphasis on how people treat each other than on their beliefs. According to its statement of purpose, the Center's work will focus on "reaching people who have given up on organized religion" and on providing "support for congregations who embrace search, not certainty."

In June 1996, I attended a three-day forum at Trinity Cathedral in Columbia, South Carolina, sponsored by the Center: "Out of the Whirlwind: Claiming a Vision of Progressive Christianity." The purpose was to bring together people from diverse backrounds with a common interest in helping to define and start a new progressive Christian movement. About one hundred attended—clergy and lay, black and white, young and middle-aged, gay and straight. Most were Episcopalians, but other faiths were represented. The talks covered a broad range—religion and politics, community life, recruitment, and inclusion.

The high point of the forum came on the last morning when we heard from about fifteen younger members of the group, most of them college students. Lest our expectations soar too high, a young woman who works for an ecumenical organization in Columbia reminded us of where we were: "Here in South Carolina we don't use the words 'progressive' and 'Christianity' in the same sentence." A young man from Dallas reported that gays in evangelical churches there were either staying in the closet or being thrown out as sinners. He had come to the forum to see if he had "a place at the table of progressive Christianity as a gay evangelical." I came away seeing a real need for a national organization for open churches and believing that, with the necessary support, The Center for Progressive Christianity could meet that need.

St. Mark's has been my spiritual home and most important community for fifteen years. I'm lucky to have found such a church. It isn't always a comfortable place to be. My skeptical views put me in a minority, and I sometimes feel like an outsider. But my fear that I would feel hypocritical went away early because, from the beginning, I've been open about my beliefs. I've been a full participant in the life of the church: *Gospel* editor, elected Vestry member, Sunday school teacher.

In August 1996, after chapter 14, "Community Life," was written, I was named Crab of the Year by the College of Crustaceans at the annual Fourth-of-July Crabfeast, ending a decade during which my qualifications had been unaccountably overlooked. The duties of the reigning crab are not onerous for a curmudgeon like me: make occasional crabby statements and a State of the Crab address at the next annual feast.

Am I a better person for going to church? I think so, but I can't prove it. My temper isn't as short as it used to be, but that may have happened anyway as I've grown older. St. Mark's led me to Honduras to do good works, but getting a story for this book was my main reason for going. I do believe that relationships with so many good people and a community ethic of straight dealing have done something to improve my behavior.

In April 1996, Jim Adams gave his last sermon before retiring. During the comment period, a succession of people rose to thank him for fostering their relationships with God in one way or another. As time was running out, my skeptical spirit grew restless. I raised my hand and said: "I'm afraid skepticism is getting a bad name this morning. I came to St. Mark's a skeptic, after fifteen years here I'm still a skeptic, and I expect to go to my grave a skeptic. I want to thank you, Jim, for making St. Mark's a safe place for skeptics."

Jim's response: "Time's up. Skepticism gets the last word."

Suggested Reading

Adams, James R. *So You Think You're Not Religious?* Boston: Cowley Publications, 1989.

Becker, Ernest. *The Denial of Death.* New York: Free Press, 1973.

The Book of Common Prayer. Greenwich, Conn.: Seabury Press, 1977.

Camus, Albert. *The Plague.* New York: Alfred A. Knopf, 1948.

Ford, Richard. *Independence Day.* New York: Random House, 1995.

James, William. *The Varieties of Religious Experience.* New York: Modern Library, 1929.

Joyce, James. *The Portrait of an Artist as a Young Man.* 1916. Reprint, Danbury, Conn.: Franklin Watts, 1964.

Robinson, John A. T. *Honest to God.* Philadelphia: Westminster Press, 1963.

Tillich, Paul. *The Shaking of the Foundations.* New York: Scribner's, 1948.

About the Author

James L. Kelley received a B.A. in humanities and a J.D. in law from the University of Iowa. While at the university, he developed skeptical views about traditional religious doctrines and left the Roman Catholic Church at age twenty-one. For the next twenty-five years he had no church affiliation or religious practices. Kelley became an openly skeptical member of St. Mark's Episcopal Church, Capitol Hill, Washington, D.C., in 1982, attracted mainly by its vital community life. Professionally, he worked as a lawyer for thirty years—in private practice, in teaching, with the U.S. Department of Justice, and with the Nuclear Regulatory Commission. He turned to full-time writing in 1993. His first book—*Psychiatric Malpractice: Stories of Patients, Psychiatrists, and the Law*—was published by Rutgers University Press in 1996. James Kelley lives in Takoma Park, Maryland.